I0141008

Men Are Too
CALLOUS
& Women Are
TOO SMART!

#LetsFixIt

Philosopher 'X'

Contents

ABOUT THE AUTHOR

Philosopher 'X'

A Therapist, Philosopher, Civil Activist, Lecturer, and Author – 'X' genuinely loves humanity. Having had the opportunity to travel and get to know people from all walks of life, Philosopher 'X' has developed many fascinating and intimate insights into the workings of society and relationships. Creating education practices that can solve current problematic life issues, this exciting and informative book offers valuable knowledge in the arena of human study and understanding.

Originally born in Mississippi, Philosopher 'X' now resides in Atlanta, Georgia, U.S.A., where he continues his therapy practice, along with frequent local television and radio appearances, and donates countless hours of volunteer charity work for the betterment of human-kind.

DEDICATION

I dedicate this book to my loving Mother, Mary Helen, who has always been a constant source of inspiration and delicious home cooked meals. I love you Mama! Also to my late Father, the "Great Riley Martin" (www.rileymartin.com) writer of the cult classic book, "*The Coming of Tan*", and the outspoken host of the hugely popular "Riley Martin Show" on Sirius/XM Radio Station 101. Thanks for your love & support! Love you Pops! R.I.P.

Introduction

First, Congratulations! By acquiring this book you're already on your way to greater, better, more loving and meaningful relationships! Why? Because you seek the knowledge and tools to make your relationships a wonderfully ecstatic reality! At the very least, change your relationships way better than they are now.

Thank You Very Much!

"The first step toward change is awareness. The second step is acceptance."

Quote ~ Nathanial Branden

I am Philosopher 'X', but you can call me "X": I'm a mid-life American Male, but I consider myself a citizen of the world. I'm a professional healer, therapist, social scientist, and philosopher. I have seen a lot of intimate relationships come and go during my time lifetime. Not only in my professional and personal life, but also with my family, friends, co-workers, celebrities, holy men and holy Women, politicians in fact, every sort of person including tweens, teens, adults, and the elderly. What gives? What's the reason for these myriads of social disconnects that seem to be plaguing the finer institutions of meaningful, long lasting relationships? Why are people stalking, filing restraining orders, and resorting to domestic violence which is running rampant daily?

Currently "relationship problems" are at an all-time high in our modern civilized society. What possesses us as educated loving people to build relations on a house of cards, rather than on a stable foundation of integrity and truth? Why are we at war with our lifemates?

I've had my share of horrible relationships – believe me it does not bear repeating. Even though I still have issues every now and then - they're not as bitingly harsh and long lasting as they once were. So, I'm passing on my many years of knowledge to you, so you also can be effective and successful in your relationship pursuits.

It seems that most of us are going into a new relationship or we're currently already in a relationship, or we're quickly moving out of a bad relationship, or we've become just plain frustrated with the entire concept of the relationship scene altogether.

So, because of our relationship involvements, (or lack thereof), it seems like people are always experiencing unfavorable, pitiful, sad relationship results either before, during, or after the hooking-up and breaking-up relationship stages.

As a philosopher, I tend to look at life from all angles to better discern, learn, and interpret the facts, variables, and circumstances that tend to construct our world of relationships.

Having and creating great relationships is like requiring and learning any other life skills. SUCCESS in relationships requires study and practice. This book will assist you in doing that.

In this book, I wish to pose and answer the following questions:

How is it that we love each other in relationships (with all our heart), then, when we have relationship problems with each other we let love turn into hate with such reckless abandon? As if we never even loved or cared about the former love interest at all?

How can we become more relatable, civilized, compassionate, and compromising in pursuit of caring relationships?

Can we be in long-lasting relationships or is that an old-fashioned myth, or modern-day folklore?

Can't we positively compromise or negotiate the terms we desire to create in our relationships without losing what we love most about our life?

Are men too callous, and women too smart for relationships to work long term?

What's Callous: cal·lous (kăl′əs) - *adjective*:

1. Having calluses; toughened: callous skin on the elbow.

2. Emotionally hardened; unfeeling: a callous indifference to the suffering of others.

To make or become callous.

Source: thefreedictionary.com

What's Smart: smart \\'smärt\\ - *adjective*:

: very good at learning or thinking about things

: showing intelligence or good judgment

: behaving or talking in a rude or impolite way: showing a lack of respect for   someone

: making one smart: **causing a sharp stinging**

Source: Merriam-Webster.com

Men tend to view women as *Smart-Alecks*, or *Know-It-All's* that are too demanding, disrespectful, and never able to be satisfied with what they already have to offer. (It's never good enough!). Women tend to view men as callous, mean-spirited, selfish, and too willing to run out and find love somewhere else. (You're so selfish!).

WHY? Read and find out the reasons for this eternal conflict between the opposite sexes.

CHAPTER 1

THE ANATOMY OF RELATIONSHIPS

Mankind has existed in modern form for at least 100,000 years and that means there have been a lot of relationships throughout human history. Countless intimate liaisons have helped spawn well over 7 billion of the most brilliant species in the known universe. You! Homo sapiens, in the Latin tongue, means 'the wise human'. The family units of our ancient ancestors did not look the way we envisage them in today's modern societies. The closest thing to relationships in the beginning probably looked more like a pride of lions with a single dominant male commanding top priority on female breeding rights and defending that right to the death.

This stands to reason given that fossilized remains of ancient humans have an estimated lifespan of only the mid-thirties or early forties, and that short human lifespan stayed pretty much the same into the middle ages (that's tens of thousands of years). That's a very short period of living compared to modern humans today which can be double or triple the ancient lifespan amounts. Families had to be started very, very young, and being that men could not reproduce people that meant that women had to keep us going as a species. Women's gestation period to incubate and give birth to a healthy baby is nine months. So, it probably worked in our ancestor's favor to have multi-partnered relationships due to the early lifespan mortality rates in adults as well as children.

In ancient times reserving time for courtship, evaluating what hobbies you had in common, *do you love me - or do I love you*, and how much have you earned financially, were probably low and not important on the relationship hook-up list that people tend to go by in modern society. Unfortunately, even today much of ancient mans' biologically ingrained DNA and genetics still carry the desire to reproduce with multiple female partners regardless of the current societal norms. Scientific tests prove that today's men, living in a highly competitive world, produce more testosterone (the I-must-compete - biological libido enhancing callous drug for men), causing men to aggressively become more aroused towards females of the species. (Testosterone arouses men whether they want to be aroused or not! It's biological.).

When successful men reach high plateaus in their career or other important life milestones, their testosterone levels skyrocket causing the males to become uber-callous in the reproduction area by a biological relationship process that's no fault of their own. This biological hiccup leads men to become easily, increasingly prone to commit infidelities when it comes to their marriages and relationships. Oddly enough, the most successful men seem to attract flocks of adoring women because relationship surveys show that many women are wildly attracted to men that exhibit confidence, wealth, and power. Who's to blame for this biological stimulator of anguish in relationships? Is it our ancestors, or our Creator that made men in such a fashion?

To View Humans as a Complexity of Paradoxes may be an understatement!

No doubt there were many variations of human family relationships in the past as civilizations along with rules and regulations changed over time. Some big reasons for changes in human relationships over time were due to male empirical societal dominance, religious dogma, access to resources such as food, water, shelter, and in some cases, female matricidal societal dominance (that means ladies were in charge).

In the Roman Empire, it was common practice to have a wife to produce an heir to the throne along with a stable of intimacy slaves - consisting of young boys, girls, men, and women to indulge the Emperor's every intimate whim. Why? Because intimacy with slaves was accepted culturally by ancient Romans and intimacy with slaves was considered non-adulterous. The Nobles and Samurai of Japan maintained one to several wives but frequented the Geisha Houses to enjoy refined painted ladies and painted men for intimate companionship. Reverend Joseph Smith, the founder of the Mormon Church, proclaimed that it was God's will to be fruitful and multiply. He had several wives until he was killed by men from a different Christian religion who said it was blasphemy to have more than one wife.

The late Queen Elizabeth, the 1st - of England, (Elizabeth was the daughter of King <u>Henry VIII,</u> and his wife <u>Queen Anne Boleyn, whom he had decapitated</u>); Queen Elizabeth reclaimed her virginity by going through a sacred ceremony so she would be seen righteous enough to rule the English people. But throughout here reign as Queen, it was widely rumored that she had a secret boyfriend that she kept secret, so that her personal relationship with her secret boyfriend wouldn't interfere with her title and position to rule her country. See, even in ancient times people gossiped about the popular celebrities!

Relationships throughout human history occasionally change one degree or another as the moral standards evolve or devolve, depending on your point of view. The most common modern form of what's considered acceptable in a marriage relationship is the one man and one woman committed relationship. People seem to want the "one on one relationship" even if the women outnumber the men and there may not be enough men alive mathematically and of suitable marriage age, to match the one–on–one perfect marriage equation. If you look at it today it seems like women in many geographical areas greatly outnumber the men. In the city of Atlanta, Georgia, the women outnumber the men at least 6 to 1---<u>6 women to every 1 man</u>; and that's only one American city. Do the math!

If there are not enough men to go around it doesn't take thinking to determine that relationship problems will arise. This often gives rise to the prospect of causing unsatisfied men to upgrade a relationship (because of the excess of women ratio), or because needy women sabotage an established relationship (because of the shortage of men), which can lead to severe relationship problems.

In relationship breakups, the offending break-uppers tend to let the chips fall where they may. Oftentimes this leads to a loss of hope and self-esteem from the person being broke up with because of feelings of betrayal and heartbreak. Relationship breakups will confuse the children of the parents splitting apart and this scenario oftentimes creates torn and bitter emotions in the children because they can think they were part of the cause of the break-up. (Children often feel stuck in the middle because they love and care about both parents).

Also, many complex hardships can arise by becoming a single-parent, such as; violent uncontrollable emotional outbursts from feelings of being overwhelmed by increased parenting responsibilities, damaged egos from thinking *I was not good enough* to stay in a relationship, shock from loss of financial resources, shock for having to live in areas with a lower standard of living, and chronic depression arising from feelings of failure and abandonment. Wow! That's a tall order of grief for what was once considered the love of your life, now dubbed a monstrous pariah! Now let's look at why we want to be in relationships in the first place...

CHAPTER 2

WHY MEN GO TO WAR

So, you find yourself chuckling over the title of this book – Men Are Too Callous and Women Are Too Smart; #LetsFixIt. I know it's a bit funny but it's very serious as well. Why? What do you think is the driving reason that causes men to go to war and kill literally millions of people? Is it for Money? Is it for Oil?

The reason men submit themselves over to the horrid brutality of war is that they hope that they can acquire money, power, and resources so that they can acquire reproduction rights from females. So, if you're a female - that means access to you! Men do almost everything (good and evil), in this world (whether they know it or not), pretty much in the hopes that either by choice or by force, they can gain access to their feminine objects of intimate desire.

The world is literally in a constant state of war so that guys' can get girls'! Now this doesn't mean that men aren't capable of having truly loving and spiritual relationships with women. On the contrary, if a man is good, and his intentions are honest and righteous, he'll make a great mate. Everything in life has a yin and yang, a good and bad, a right and wrong aspect to it. Relationships encompass that duality as well. That's why understanding human relationships are of the highest importance so that we can better understand each other, and stop warring with each other.

CHAPTER 3

UNDERSTANDING THE HUMAN BRAIN

What has made us jump to the top of the food-chain, make blockbuster movies, join political parties and countless other activities? You guessed it, the three-pound universe, also known as the Brain. The brain is a fantastic organ and it's the place where our intellectual, psychological, and emotional activities take place. Electrochemical responses govern the brain's activities, which are in turn greatly influenced by our outer environment. No one knows for certain the numbers, but it's estimated that our brains contain roughly 86 billion brain cells. A piece of brain tissue the size of a grain of sand contains 100,000 neurons, and 1 billion synapses, all communicating with each other in perfect unison. Wow!

FACT: Do you know that the reason you're who and what you consider yourself to be is because of the people you've associated with in your life. Especially the people responsible for your upbringing as a child.

In other words, its other people supplying you with their available data that helped you determine who you are, and what you will potentially become, by selectively feeding you the information they wanted you to grow up into. Only when you grow older do you purposely decide what type of person you will become, but for the most part your direction in life - such as tastes in food, fashion, religion, concepts of right and wrong, etc. was chosen for you by other people. From the very day you were born. You had no choice because you had no knowledge that you had a choice. We eagerly followed the lead of those providing love and attention, (in some cases abuse), in our young impressionable lives.

The way our brain works, is that our social circles must reinforce who and what we are, otherwise we'd be in a constant state of psychological confusion. Many people perform poorly in life because they were taught (programmed), in overly dramatized negative behavior and not enough positive mental behavior. Proper philosophical and emotional control tactics to develop life and people skills were not introduced to most people. So, people suffer a lot of bad relationships and life situations from lack of knowledge. Unfortunately, our societies and schools gladly teach us how to learn and make money and we get stuck with hoping that this job education will lead us to emotional happiness--- but this is often not the case. Whether you're rich or poor, you'll still encounter relationship problems that require you to possess specific skills to successfully resolve the problematic issues that certainly will arise.

Take the case of Feral (Wild) Children: Believe it or not there have been children literally raised by wolves in the wild. Hard to believe, I know. Because of most of the information (mental data programming), the wild children received from the wolf clan, they believed, thought, hunted, and acted like their canine relatives and friends. Grrrrrr! After the Feral Children were captured and numerous attempts were made to educate the wild children (by the best psychological teachers available in their day), to assimilate them back into human society, all the attempts to re-educate the children unfortunately failed.

Every attempt failed because of the limited data received by their young developing brains in the earliest stages of their childhood. Their brains had become intellectually underdeveloped and totally lost the ability to properly absorb how to be a normal human and process information like our brains can. This fact caused the Feral Children to be forever wild, unchangeable, and unprogrammable. The scientific term associated with the ability to program, alter, add, or change the way we think is called "neuroplasticity".

It's important that you understand clearly, without a doubt, that the bulk of what you know and act upon in your life daily is still largely determined by what others in your immediate environment taught you about yourself, and about life, good or bad. I hope whoever cared for you in your early childhood told you that you're beautiful, smart, kind, and that you can accomplish anything you wanted to in life. If not, your brain may be lacking the appropriate brain cells to easily learn things which may make it complicated to learn new data. But fear not! Science has proven that in most cases even if you lack certain brain smarts, if you're diligent, you can learn new helpful things. Learning difficult subjects just takes more practice and time to retain new and different information in the brain.

To be able to retain what you learn and have it stick requires persistence and repetition, (that means you must go over the subject you wish to learn over, and over, and over again, until it sticks). So, even I can learn how to speak a new language; which is not that easy for me my friends. **(Only repetition of thought can re-program your brain).** Consciously knowing how your thought processes came into existence, whether good or bad, affords you the opportunity to change the way you think - for the better. A lot of the things you do are not entirely your fault; your brain has been placed in a box by others from the very first day you were born.

If you chose, you can introduce new and more helpful thoughts into your mind by exploring self-help information, (like this book), that will vanquish old problematic thoughts that bind you to frustration, anger, violence, and the financial struggle to make ends meet. If you are truly determined and willing to deliberately create positive thoughts that will shift you away from producing negativity and terrible outcomes in your life, I guarantee you that within 1-3 years you will be living a successful golden life because you changed the possibilities of your future outcomes. That's thinking outside the box!

"The best way to predict the future is to create it."

Quote ~ Abraham Lincoln

It's not impossible to think outside the box! In fact, it's a necessary life skill to be able to think outside the box. You can learn how to understand your personal hopes, wants, needs, and desires that will in turn, show you how to be compassionate, loving, understanding, and to civilly compromise in your relationships with others---which will lead you on the path of a more peaceful and happy life; Right Now! You will learn to accept love and give love to your mate without feeling that it's a sign of weakness or an unpardonable love disease that makes you vulnerable within your personal relationships.

Every emotion or feeling you have is a combination of brain chemicals being transmitted throughout the brain by millions of electrical currents. These chemicals create your world by allowing you to experience your life emotions from love to hate and everything in-between. I could go on teaching you about the number of cells and other interesting brain tidbits, but let's get to the heart, or brain of the matter. ☺

"Everything you love or like about life,
Is varying stages of physiological,
And psychological addiction." *Philosopher 'X'*

Everything that makes you happy, (big or small), affects the brain as some stage of brain addiction. Only some actions, substances, and objects create bigger, more desired pleasurable responses than others. Addiction is a double-edged sword that can be used for good or bad. What's the greatest addiction in the world? Love of course! Secondly, closely followed by the burning desire to be right all the time about every little thing. Love reigns supreme! Love is the most powerful substance in brain addiction. We all need LOVE. Crimes of passion and scandals tend to make the headlines because of the drama and entertainment value. Rule #1 of news broadcasting – if it bleeds it leads. Why is this important?

Because people are addicted to people! People are addicted to people like a crack addict is addicted to rock cocaine. Take away the crack and you have one volatile, jittery, and angry individual looking for a fix, or a robbery to get money to pay for a fix (a fix means to buy drugs to satiate your drug habit). I'll elaborate more on this subject of people addiction in a later chapter. Good or evil, big or small, everyone needs to be loved. Over seven billion love children prove that people want to be loved - *a lot*. Be that as it may: If Love is the biggest addiction what's its opposite? The thing which causes negative unloving behavior?

The opposite of love is rejection and hate! People would rather risk death many times rather than being rejected by family, peers, and people they have crushes on… and that's a scientific fact. Teens would risk death or prison to preserve their friendship and top swagger status with their peers, people will stay in bad marriages and suffer domestic abuse rather than lose their political, religious, societal, or family status. People are literally horrified to speak in public forums due to this powerful fear of rejection. We're interesting beings, there's no doubt about that. When we were born, we had a relatively clean mental slate, except for one basic mental program we are all born with:

The Survival Program provides – I am to live as long as I can with as little discomfort as possible.
This one sentence of mental programming tends to rule the entire world! Philosopher'X'

Just think about it for a minute…

Why do you date a certain type or race, look to marry someone who's achieved financial success, socialize in certain societal circles, pick a job, choose a religion, exercise or not to exercise, go to a college, spend outrageous amounts of money on products to look good, hate to be proven wrong about certain subjects, change your hair and clothing styles, and sometimes get plastic surgery?

Read the survival program sentence again:

I am to live as long as I can with as little discomfort as possible.

We are programmed from birth about wishing to pattern everything in our lives to extend and enhance our lives. We all hope to live a long comfortable life - period! Why is this important? People tend to limit their choices in relationships entirely based on automatic subconsciously programmed behavior, without even knowing it. People that are not aware of this fact never press beyond preconceived survival notions and imagined delusions of grandeur to take a risk outside the box which would most likely lead them to the happiness they seek. In other words: You block your blessings!

I, Philosopher 'X' conclude that if lovelorn people are to overcome their preconceived, prejudicial programmed differences; People must become a more united species that's willing to gain an objective mental understanding of our biological and psychological tendencies or we may never have peace and love occur in our lives. After all isn't that what we desperately long to have – Peace and Love? I love the idea of humanity obtaining Universal Unconditional Love – but that's just me.

**"The opposite of addiction is not sobriety,
The opposite of addiction is connection.
The core of addiction is about not wanting
to be present in your life because your life
is too painful to be in."**

Quote ~ *Author* ~ *Johann Hari*

CHAPTER 4

THE BRAIN PART 2

No, we're not finished with looking at that fat jelly-filled organ between your ears. There's a reason why we walk around with all sorts of mental issues, thinking inside, instead of outside the box, and obsessing over *I am right - you are wrong* issues:

Cognitive dissonance is an uncomfortable feeling caused by holding two contradictory ideas simultaneously. The "ideas" or "cognitions" in question may include attitudes and beliefs, the awareness of one's behavior, and facts. The theory of cognitive dissonance proposes that people have a motivational drive to reduce dissonance by changing their attitudes, beliefs, and behaviors, or by justifying or rationalizing their attitudes, beliefs, and behaviors. Cognitive dissonance theory is one of the most influential and extensively studied theories in social psychology.

Dissonance normally occurs when a person perceives a logical inconsistency among his or her cognitions. This happens when one idea implies the opposite of another. For example, a belief in animal rights could be interpreted as inconsistent with eating meat or wearing fur. Noticing the contradiction leads to dissonance, which could be experienced as anxiety, guilt, shame, anger, embarrassment, stress, and other negative emotional states. When people's ideas are consistent with each other, they're in a state of harmony, or *consonance*. If cognitions are unrelated, they're categorized as *irrelevant* to each other and do not lead to dissonance.

A powerful cause of dissonance is an idea in conflict with a fundamental element of the self-concept, such as "I'm a good person" or "I made the right decision." The anxiety that comes with the possibility of having made a bad decision can lead to rationalization, the tendency to create additional reasons or justifications to support one's choices. A person who just spent too much money on a new car might decide that the new vehicle is much less likely to break down than his or her old car. This belief may or may not be true, but it would likely reduce dissonance and make the person feel better. Dissonance can also lead to confirmation bias, the denial of disconfirming evidence, and other ego defense mechanisms.

SOURCE: Wikipedia.com

To get a proper understanding of what I'm saying here: When people have confronted that their position is not true and they continue to deny the facts with evidence proving them wrong right before their eyes, rather than admitting to being wrong, humans purposely deny the facts no matter what. The brain begins producing chemicals called 'opiates' to be released that make it feel good inside your mind to be right--- even if you're defending a false, unnerving truth. A famous filmmaker stated, "He doesn't know if mankind can survive with that kind of illogical reaction because it falsely overrules factually reasonable thought!" Another astute person stated that we suffer from the disease of having to be right all the time.

Being proven wrong should be a reason to celebrate because now you can know the right answer and be more enriched and empowered in your life from knowing the facts. People, it's ok to be wrong! It's been said by many cultures for many years that <u>knowledge is power</u>. We're never taught in schools that it's ok to be wrong, and that each wrong answer can bring you one step closer to the truth. You get bad grades when you're wrong in school and that's not the best way to teach our children and adults.

In Finland, the schools used to have identical low scholastic aptitude tests nearly identical to the low IQ statistics held by the students in the United States. Now Finland's students are the number one smartest children in the world! When the Finnish teachers were asked how they got their children to be so smart – the Finnish said the following:

1. We stopped giving children tests.

2. We stopped giving the children homework assignments, we have the children complete their tasks in class and free up their time to enjoy their home life.

3. We placed a great deal of emphasis on the children developing personal creativity.

4. We shortened the children's school hours to four instead of eight hours.

5. We made each class subject fun to learn to keep the children interested and focused on learning.

I think we can learn a lot from Finland in the Child Education Department.

The Rise and Fall of Human Intelligence

Take note that everything that you may feel in any kind of way (i.e. love, hate, laughter, arousal, memories, thinking, that little voice you always hear in your head, etc.) can only occur in your mind with a physical electrochemical reaction happening first. In other words, it's physical chemical reactions in the brain that enables us to catch a ball or drink a cup of coffee. Electrochemical reactions are a series of lightning fast reactions which occur almost instantaneously in your mind, making it possible for you to feel and experience what you feel and think about. Also, if what you're thinking about is good or bad.

The same goes for intelligence because your IQ (Intelligence Quotient), is dependent on a certain chemical produced in your head that will determine if your IQ will be up (smart), or down (not-so-smart). The IQ depends on the production and transmission of this brain chemical known as **Tryptophan Hydroxylase. Do you know what happens inside your brain when you have any negative emotions like anger, hate, envy, jealousy, fear etc.?**

Negative emotions cause a lack of production of Tryptophan Hydroxylase to occur in the brain - causing you to become a bit stupid. A great deal of what makes up your intelligence is dependent on the flow of Tryptophan Hydroxylase inside your brain. Negative emotions affect the logical thinking processes of the mind causing you to say and do very selfish and harmful things to either yourself or someone else (especially people you're close too). This irreverent use of passionate emotions may cause sweet little you to use foul language, destroy someone's personal property (like cars), or physically fighting someone; which can lead to the ultimate crime of passion - murder.

Seriously, you effectively give up all logical reasoning to negative emotions when you're angry. **A negative thought only has power if you ACT On It!** If you choose to ignore the bad thoughts they will soon fade away from your mind but if you dwell on them they will grow into the monsters that destroy lives. If you don't want negative reactions to negative emotions to drive you off a cliff, then you must take fast action not to give destructive unhealthy thoughts power over you. As humans we're simply not taught to deal with these negative mental chemical responses in our scholastic institutions which are supposed to supply us with the tools to prepare us for life and relationships. This is a modern-day horror story that we must change. Now for your edification, I present to you the ultimate mental tool that I personally invented to stop the loss of intelligence before it ruins your day, week, year, or life. Just this exercise alone will be worth the price of this book! Oh, and yes, I do use this tool and it works!

Keep the Peace - Mental Control Exercise (MCE)

Scenario: A violent argument ensues:

It was my parking spot first! Can you stop talking on the phone, I paid to see this movie! I think he's a terrorist! I don't have the money for that bill right now! You're so stupid, I don't know why they even let you come to school! Get out of my way idiot! Tough situations. When you're confronted with tough and challenging situations (and there'll be many); ask yourself this one simple yet profound question: **"Is this an immediate threat to my life?"**

Then answer the question in your head. Ask yourself and answer back! Say a mental 'No' if your life isn't immediate danger! Then tell yourself, (this is literal), to relax and calm down, as it's not worth the trouble, or better still, chill the heck out! Ask and answer this question repeatedly when faced with negativity and don't stop until you calm yourself down. It stops your intelligence chemical levels falling completely down and prevents you from doing something harmful or stupid.

Anger is an electro-chemical-physical response! I don't care who you are, what education you have, or lack of education thereof, MCE will work to calm your anger down from the shortcomings that make us idiots from time to time. Most of the situations that we react badly too are not life threatening at all. But our brains react as if we are about to be splatted on the windshield like a bug. That's another trait we picked up from our cave-dwelling ancestors, who undoubtedly had to run for their lives almost every day from saber-toothed tigers trying to turn them into lunch. That's why we stress out and feel so terrible during these spasmodic episodes.

The quicker you act to resolve the matter by questioning it, the better off you will be. You'll learn how to be peaceful in seconds. Whereas other people may need a lifetime of couch therapy to cope with mental stress. Remember this takes practice! I invented it and I still must use it to keep calm when I'm driving in big city traffic. But it gets easier as you go along. It's a life tool that can save your life. There're way too many good people locked away in prisons that wished they knew this mental technique before the door of freedom slammed shut on them because of a stupid act that only took seconds to ruin their lives. Some mistakes will cause you to suffer for a lifetime. Please don't let that be you. You're better than that. **Remember During Tough Times Ask: "<u>Is this an immediate threat to my life?</u>"**

Lists of Foods That Nourish and Strengthen the Brain

<u>Water</u> - The brain is approximately 80 percent water so proper hydration is key. A lack of water can cause the brain to shrink and not function properly. A good way to measure intake is half your body weight in ounces daily and more if you work out vigorously or live in hot climates. 60 percent of the brain is fat (it's the fattest part of your body), so you need to eat foods with healthy fats (Omegas 3's and 6's), to keep your brain happy such as oatmeal, fish oil (salmon, tuna, etc.) walnuts, almonds, and other nuts (raw nuts are good sometimes), avocados, extra virgin olive oil, coconut oil, hemp seed oil, flax seed or flax seed oil.

Take one, 100 percent Multi-Vitamin a day. I sometimes take multi-vitamins once every other day as it saves money and the vitamins last longer. It's a great idea to include vitamin supplements in your diet especially if you don't eat lots of fresh fruits and vegetables daily. I strongly recommend them once you pass the age of 40 years old. Foods high in vitamins and antioxidants such as red bell peppers, spinach, oranges (not juice, eat oranges with some of the white pith by peeling it with a knife), broccoli, tomatoes, basically salad vegetables (generally fruits and veggies with bright colors). Eat them raw sometimes if possible, so that you receive the added health benefits of raw enzymes (heating fruits and veggies past 110 degrees can destroy healthy enzymes). *(For more info about brain health see BrainMDHealth.com ~ Dr. Daniel Amen).*

Other Ways to Keep Your Brain Healthy

1. Get at least six hours of sleep a day. Some low-caffeine teas can help you sleep, and try to avoid caffeinated products at least six hours prior to bedtime.

2. Avoid toxic skin care products and don't use toxic cleaning chemicals without protective clothing (read the product labels for dangers).

3. Try natural remedies when possible, like herbs and holistic treatments, but check to see if they are safe from your doctor, especially if you're on prescription meds. Limit your over-the-counter and prescription meds if you don't need them to maintain your health. Too much medication tends to stress the internal organs (especially the liver), which can lead to greater health problems down the road.

4. Avoid injuring your head at all costs! Always wear your seat belt and if you're biking, climbing, or participating in any other hazardous sports, make sure your head is protected with the appropriate head gear. A brain injury can destroy your life by creating mental health issues or limited mobility, etc.... In many brain injuries, the damage done is irreversible. Be smart.

5. Obesity causes you to age faster and can stress the mind by inhibiting the body of proper circulatory function and adequate nutrition absorption. For every 15 pounds, you are overweight. (15 pounds is the average weight of a bowling ball), you put

a blanket of pressure on and around your internal organs. Too much pressure on the internal organs greatly weakens the organ's capabilities to function properly. Your internal organs are basically moist balloon-filled sacs made-up of proteins that take care of specific body functions. Added weight squashes the soft balloons, so to speak. Keep your weight at a healthy size, which means you don't have to be bone skinny, but not too big and heavy. Treat your body with respect and it will make you smile.

6. <u>**Find Ways To Relive Your Stress – Stress Kills**</u>! Too much stress in the brain and body translates to a life loaded with excessive health pains and problems. As a Massage Therapist and a former military hospital aid worker, I know the ravaging harms of what too much stress can do to a human being. Stress is majorly destructive. If not treated and reduced it will eventually get the better of you and probably kill you dead. Treatments such as therapeutic body massage, yoga, moderate exercise, personal relaxation down-time (quality time for yourself), and relaxing meditation are essential tools in the battle to reduce life stressors.

WHAT STRESS CAN DO TO YOUR RELATIONSHIPS?

Did You Know, That When you're in a Relationship Your Health and Well-being Directly Affects Your

Partners Joyful Quality of Life.

Problems Created From Stressors:

a. Chronic Illnesses – hypertension (high blood pressure), cancer, cystic tumors, migraine headaches, auto-immune diseases, chronic muscle spasms and pain, neuropathy (nerve pain), more susceptible to flues and colds, stomach ulcers, GERD (Gastro Esophageal Reflux Disease), vaginal dryness, male impotence, premature ejaculation, etc...

b. Stresses can cause – premature hair loss, aging of the skin, acne outbreaks, lack of sleep, severe depression, moodiness, etc.…

c. Violent crimes – suicides, murders, rapes, robberies, road rage, etc.…

d. ***Did you know that when you're stressed-out it's impossible to digest your food?*** Food can sit in your stomach and intestines for hours, even days when you're under stress; which means your health will suffer greatly. Health problems will arise from insufficient nutrition, bowel toxicity, and a lowered immune system. So, find ways to keep stress away! Your brain and body will thank you for it, and so will your life partners.

Exercising the Body - Exercises the Brain

Did You Know, That Brain Function and Memory Increases When You Exercise On a Regular Basis? Very true!

Exercise is key to great brain health. Brisk walking for 10-30 minutes - three to four times a week can make a huge difference to your healthy long-term brain integrity (so park your vehicle a distance away sometimes and walk).

You don't have to spend all day toiling away in a gym – unless you want to. Another great exercise is having a great intimacy life. It improves overall wellbeing, bonding, memory, and stress relief so be safe and have fun. Make your hobbies part of your exercise, such as hiking, biking, martial arts training, bowling, skating, dancing, etc. This is a great way to keep your body beautiful healthy and strong and makes for a happy brain in la <u>Cabeza,</u> (that's Spanish for the head).

"Life is about earning more, living more, and giving more!"

Quote ~ John Assaraf ~ Brain Training Specialist
~ Access2Success.com

CHAPTER 5

ARE MEN TOO CALLOUS & WOMEN TOO SMART?

Well, are men too callous? Can they keep their privates in check long enough to have sustainable long lasting and meaningful relationships? This premise has been a bane (problem), to societies all over the world for centuries. Many lives seemingly have been ruined by the fruits and seeds of the male loins. From Presidents, to Professional Athletes, what can be done to stop this testosterone scourge that tears the hearts out of unsuspecting women in relationships with men? I, Philosopher 'X' am very much a man. I'll attempt to answer this question by opening this dialog with the following true life story:

My Family Story

My Grandfather John, was a tough, no nonsense man. John remained married to my lovely Grandmother Dolly and he remained faithful to her all his life. Approximately 15 years after my Grandfather's death our family learned that Grandfather had an older son in a previous marriage relationship that we knew nothing about. Did this secretive relationship happen before his marriage to my Grandma? Maybe or maybe not? We don't know for sure. My family will never know why his first-born son, (also named John), was kept a secret from us.

Now I have a great new Uncle that gave me nice gifts when I visited him in Chicago but my family would have liked to have known about Uncle John sooner, and Uncle John would have liked to have known about his biological father while he was still alive. Amazingly, there are countless secret relationship stories with similar unknown child themes throughout history. Many married people knew of their previous secret coital situations but choose to remain in their marriage and maintain the hidden skeletons in their closets hoping that no one would find out. Especially family members.

Often people refer to the good old days when Grandpa stayed married and did not stray, but stray many men did, and for whatever reasons it was felt best to keep secret liaisons and love children away from the immediate families' knowledge. Such scenes have played out in families across the world seemingly forever and I don't know if men or women will ever stop outside relations to resemble the ideal moral religious molds that many people claim to aspire to…except maybe for Hugh Hefner (Renowned International Playboy), he seems to be politically correct in his exemption from the rule of monogamous fidelity.

What causes this Philandering behavior?

- Beginning in early childhood, (culturally), men learn that it is considered macho to be a womanizing stud, and have relations with many women.

- Man's strong biological urges to be engaged with many women still exist in the DNA, (remember running around and looking for love in high school).

- Feeling rejection by their prospective spouses can exacerbate male intimacy urges causing men to seek outside affection.

- Being a highly successful businessman causes men's testosterone to skyrocket greatly increasing intimacy urges.

Are men too callous? Yes, but we can change.

Men, we must stop abusing women by deceiving them with lies, ulterior motives, and emotional and physical abuse. Why? Because abuse by men trains our once loving ladies to become callous and bitter people... and hurt people, *hurt* people. Time to Man-Up! Time to be honest about what we're up to or we'll never live in a more harmonious human society. Truly Men, stop the generation-after-generation of womanizing corruption and show the world what it means to be a real Man. **A real Man is honest about what he wants out of a relationship, even if it's hard.**

Are Women too smart?

Women have been fighting men for equality for what seems like an eternity. It's not been easy in this world for women, yet they still hang out with the guys and even have intimate relations with men every now and then. That of course, has helped with the current population explosion. In Ancient Egypt, women had more equal rights than other ancient societies and could divorce their men when they wanted to without being stoned, publicly shunned, or burned alive. It has taken over 2000 years for equality rights to be retained in modern society by determined, courageous women. Strong women who weren't willing to take no for an answer. The Divine Feminine.

Today's modern woman can work any job, get the best education, pick who she wants to love, run businesses, and be political leaders in the highest offices of the land. I applaud you ladies! To be able to do all this and still find time to have babies and be mothers'. That's nothing short of miraculous! It's a new day in the world formally dominated by men in nearly all aspects of life. Now women have regained a lot of power and there's a new sheriff in town, high heels and all! I applaud your extraordinary bravery and talents Ladies! Bravo! Women's ability to adapt, assimilate, and overcome the evils of patriarchal social injustice is truly inspiring.

The Little Rock Nine

A fellow author once said to me, "I grew up in racist Little Rock, Arkansas, and I went to Little Rock Central High School during the late 1950's. That's when nine black students were first segregated into my school. I didn't understand why my fellow white students, friends, and family members hated black people so much? So, I asked my uncle, who was working as an anti-segregation attorney for the city of Birmingham at the time to block the segregation into the city's schools, "What's so bad about negroes going to the same school as whites?" My uncle told me that if we allow the blacks to become equals in our society they'll have intimate misogynistic relationships with our daughters!"

The author didn't take her uncle's answer very serious and figured that her uncle didn't want to tell her the whole story because of her youth, and his important social status in the community. Mentally she conceded that it must be for economic reasons, or because of a longstanding system of race hatred passed down from generations by ignorant, hateful white extremists.

Thirty years later while researching and writing her book about the Little Rock 9, she asked her uncle, (the anti-segregation lawyer), the same question again, "I don't understand why my fellow white students, friends and family members hated black people so much?" Her uncle said angrily, "See I told you that colored race mixing would happen!" She then stated, "Oh my goodness! That's when I finally realized that it was about controlling the bodies of white women and that violent reactions towards the black people by angry white protestors were attempts to stop interracial race-mixing."

The Muslim Story

I, 'X', didn't realize the significance of what the author of the *Little Rock Nine* told me at that time until I saw a documentary about a Muslim British citizen, who was inundated with multiple death threats by an Islamic extremist. He claimed he'd survived two assassination attempts against him by his Muslim community that prompted the British government to issue him bodyguards for his protection.

This Muslim man claimed that he was peacefully working to end terrorist extremism and acquire equal rights for Islamic women in his British country and throughout the Middle East. The Muslim gentlemen stated that much of the oppression and terror being perpetrated on innocent men, women, and children by other Muslims was committed in the name of Islam. When this Muslim gentleman was asked by a western news interviewer, "Why did so many traditional Muslims condone and justify violent behavior to be taken against non-Muslims, as well as their own people?" The Muslim gentlemen said, "That everything the extremist do is about controlling the lives of Muslim women, not the noble cause of defending their people from harm!" That's when I had my OMG (Oh My God) moment! All this crazy, selfish, barbaric male behavior is about keeping the women regulated, controlled, and in-check!

Remember the story I told you about my grandfather in the beginning of this chapter? A comedian once stated, "Men are only as faithful in a relationship as they can be." The truth is, men have been philandering for centuries. (Philandering is defined as to have casual or illicit intimate relations with a woman or with many women; *especially* to be unfaithful to one's wife). I conclude that if women in the past were not copasetic (by choice or by force), with the philandering, "How could men carry on their philandering ways throughout human history?

The Survival Program – which states I need to live as long as I can with as little discomfort as possible.

Being unenlightened, men always seemed to dictate what roles women should play in society (as well as other men). Men had a stranglehold on what a women's quality of life would or could ever be, during ancient times. Now, in this new day and time, women are highly educated, demand a better quality of life, and they demand more loyalty, morality, and commitment from the men they wish to have relationships with…no matter what influences the males' libido, socially or biologically.

Modern women proudly state, "I am smart, I am beautiful, I am strong, I have my own money, I drive my own car, I own my own home, and I don't have to take this crap from you anymore! I don't need a man! I can do bad all by myself! I am Woman hear me Roar!" Raaaahhh! So, this is where the proverbial crap hits the fan! In which:

Men are too callous & Women are too smart?

There's been a paradigm shift in the way society exist now with modern women being strategically demanding and powerful with their relationship choices, and lustful men wishing that they can still have their cake and eat it too.

What is a Paradigm Shift? *Noun*

- : An important change that happens when the usual way of thinking about or doing something is replaced by a new and different way *<This discovery will bring about a paradigm shift in our understanding of evolution.>*

Source: Merriam-Webster.com

This mental shift was thousands of years in the making. Increments of progress by generations of women's accomplishments, failures, and time. Changes have been made for better and for worse depending on your personal point of view. Families are being split apart by relationship problems every minute of every day. Relationships between families, communities and congress have been deteriorating at a rate never seen before in our lifetimes. Do you ever get the feeling that even though you're in a room with a million people, you're still alone? Feeling emotionally detached (i.e. loneliness, depression, misunderstood), has hit epidemic proportions in society. People turn to drugs, intimacy, and treating people like scum to attempt to ease their pain, but this is only a temporary fix. I want everyone to be happy in their relationships because life is so short.

Time is one thing you can never get back. With all the dangers and stresses we deal with daily, "can't we all just get along!?"

CHAPTER 6

POST–TRAUMATIC STRESS DISORDER (PTSD)

Why have I included a chapter on PTSD; most commonly known as an affliction of Veterans of War?

Being a Philosopher and a U.S. Army Veteran, I was curious to know why PTSD is such a debilitating disorder to my military peers. Let's look at this mental disease more closely brothers and sisters:

Post-traumatic stress disorder: A common anxiety disorder that develops after exposure to a terrifying event or ordeal in which grave physical harm occurred or was threatened. Family members of victims also can develop the disorder. PTSD can occur in people of any age, including children and adolescents. More than twice as many women as men experience PTSD following exposure to trauma. Depression, alcohol or other substance abuse, or anxiety disorders frequently co-occur with PTSD.

The diagnosis of PTSD requires that one or more symptoms from each of the following categories be present for at least a month and that symptom or symptoms must seriously interfere with leading a normal life:

- Reliving the event through upsetting thoughts, nightmares, or flashbacks, or having very strong mental and physical reactions if something reminds the person of the event.

- Avoiding activities, thoughts, feelings or conversations that remind the person of the event; feeling numb to one's surroundings; or being unable to remember details of the event.

- Having a loss of interest in important activities, feeling all alone, being unable to have normal emotions or feeling that there is nothing to look forward to in the future.

- Feeling that one can never relax and must be on guard all the time to protect oneself, trouble sleeping, feeling irritable, overreacting when startled, angry outbursts or trouble concentrating.

Traumatic events that may trigger post-traumatic stress disorder (PTSD) include violent personal assaults, natural or human-caused disasters, accidents, or military combat. Among those who may experience PTSD are troops who served in the Vietnam and Gulf Wars; rescue workers involved in the aftermath of disasters like the terrorist attacks on New York City and Washington, D.C.; survivors of the Oklahoma City bombing; survivors of accidents, physical abuse, and other crimes; immigrants fleeing violence in their countries; survivors of the 1994 California earthquake, the 1997 North and South Dakota floods, and hurricanes Hugo and Andrew; and people who have witnessed traumatic events.

Many people with PTSD repeatedly re-experience the ordeal in the form of flashback episodes, memories, nightmares, or frightening thoughts, especially when they are exposed to events or objects reminiscent of the trauma. Anniversaries of the event can also trigger symptoms. People with PTSD also experience emotional numbness and sleep disturbances, depression, anxiety, and irritability or outbursts of anger. Feelings of intense guilt are also common. Most people with PTSD try to avoid any reminders or thoughts of the ordeal. PTSD is diagnosed when symptoms last more than one month.

Physical symptoms such as headaches, gastrointestinal distress, immune system problems, dizziness, chest pain, or discomfort in other parts of the body are common in people with PTSD. Often, these symptoms may be treated without the recognition that they stem from an anxiety disorder.

Treatment may be through cognitive-behavioral therapy, group therapy, and/or exposure therapy, in which the person gradually and repeatedly relives the frightening experience under controlled conditions to help him or her work through the trauma. Several types of medication, particularly the selective serotonin reuptake inhibitors (SSRIs) and other antidepressants, can also help relieve the symptoms of PTSD. Giving people an opportunity to talk about their experiences very soon after a catastrophic event may reduce some of the symptoms of PTSD. A study of 12,000 school children who lived through a hurricane in Hawaii found that those who got counseling early on were doing much better two years later than those who did not.

Source: Medicinenet.com

Bingo! I literally know hundreds of people from around the world and every one of them who's lived past the age of 16 years, has at one time suffered from, or still suffers from PTSD, including myself. Every broken heart, every failed goal, every lost fight, every divorce, everything that affects us negatively and plays back on rewind, over and over in our gelatinous filled heads! How many of us have had or wished to have the prescribed treatments needed to heal from emotionally, replayed debilitating anguish inside your head? I'm raising my hand. Treatment for most people is toughing it out alone, following bad advice from friends, reaching the bottom of a whiskey bottle, or worse!

People are literally living their lives suffering from multiple bouts of mental illness! Therefore, I strongly recommend that classes in Philosophy of Self, Philosophy of Life, and Human Relations are taught in our schools from an early age to ease much of the misery in the world. A Life Education Class that promotes peace, love, compassion and understanding between both genders. But if you're not a child, start now! It's never too late to learn and become your greatest version. Your loved ones will praise you for it. Also, it's very important that as citizens and taxpayers that we demand that help is made publicly available to people by our governing entities. The government has the funds to create specialists and facilities that can aid the people in the healing of torn emotions. Otherwise look forward to more dysfunctional families with abused children. Let's aid each other and become better people.

CHAPTER 7

THE TRUTH ABOUT RELATIONSHIPS

Being less serious let's look at some of the jokes about women and men circulating on the internet: **It's not difficult to make a woman happy. A man only needs to be...**

1. a friend	14.a stylist	27. gallant
2. a companion	15. a sexologist	28. intelligent
3. a lover	16. a gynecologist	29. funny
4.a brother	17. a exterminator	30. creative
5. a good father	18. a psychologist	31. tender
6. a master	19. a healer	32.strong
7. a chef	20.a good listener	33.understanding
8. an electrician	21. an organizer	34. tolerant
9. a carpenter	22. very clean	35. prudent
10. a plumber	23. sympathetic	36. ambitious
11. a mechanic	24. athletic	37. capable
12. a decorator	25. warm	38. courageous
13. a stylist	26. attentive	39. determined

40. true

41. wealthy

42. dependable

43. passionate

44. compassionate

45. give her compliments regularly

46. love shopping

47. be honest

48. be very rich

49. not stress her out

50. not look at other girls

51. give her lots of attention, but expect little yourself

52. give her lots of time, especially time for herself

53. give her lots of space, never worrying about where she goes

AT THE SAME TIME, YOU MUST ALSO, IT IS VERY IMPORTANT:

54. **NEVER TO FORGET:**	**HOW TO MAKE A MAN HAPPY:**
1. birthdays	1. show up naked
2. anniversaries	2. bring food

As funny as this joke may seem it's actually rooted in fact. Studies have shown through controlled surveys of thousands of men and women, that when men were asked to make a list of what they wanted and needed from a mate in their relationships the result was approximately three items long. Whereas the women being surveyed about what they wanted out of relationships with their men were regularly hundreds of items long. Ladies, I don't mean to be a prude, but I've never in the history of humanity found a man of the greatest caliber, to be that perfect. If they did exist, who were they married to and for how long?

Also, a noted female relationship author (I saw once on Oprah), conducted a survey of married women around the world, asking them "What do you want from a man in a relationship?" I will give you 3 guesses which country she found that the women were the most demanding. You guessed it - the good old USA – the United States of America. Yay number one again! Apologies for my sarcasm. ☺ If you're wondering what the men listed, it was that they loved women that genuinely liked doing things with them when hanging out with each other and that they are attractive, but not necessarily drop-dead gorgeous. Also, that women have a good sense of humor. Ladies, without being facetious on my part, "Why are you so demanding of men in relationships?"

Now - World Wide Web Jokes Circulated About Men

Q: What's the difference between E.T. and a man?
A: E.T. phoned home.

Q:How do men sort their laundry?
A: "Filthy" and "Filthy but wearable".

Q: What are two reasons why men don't mind their own business?
1. No mind
2. No business.

Q: Why are men like a can of spray paint?
A: One squeeze and they're all over you.

Q: How can you tell if your husband is dead?
A: The intimacy is the same, but you get the remote.

HUSBAND: Shall we try a different position tonight?
WIFE: That's a good idea.... you stand by the ironing board while I sit on the sofa and fart.

Q: What do you call a man who expects to have relations on the second date?
A: Slow.

Q: What is the insensitive bit at the base of the reproduction organ called?
A: The man.

Q: Why are men like blenders?
A: You need one, but you're not quite sure why ...or... They burn out if you run them too hard...

What Women Should Know About Men

1. If you think the way to a man's heart is through his stomach you're aiming too high.

2. Women don't make fools of men, most of them are the do-it-yourself types.

3. The best reason to divorce a man is a health reason: you've got sick of him.

4. Never trust a man who says he's the boss at home. He probably lies about other things too.

5. If you want a nice man, go for a bald one… they try harder.

6. Go for younger men. You might as well - they never mature anyway.

7. There are only two four letter words that are offensive to men, "don't" and "stop" (but not used together).

8. Men are all the same, they just have different faces so you can tell them apart.

9. Whenever you meet a man who would make a good husband, you will usually find that he is.

10. Scientists have just discovered something that can do the work of five men… a Woman.

11. Men's brains are like the prison system, not enough cells per man.

12. Husbands are like children, they're fine if they're someone else's.

I must admit that I find these jokes funny and sometimes true. Ok back to some serious discussion:

The truth of the matter is that throughout humankind's turbulent relationship history, relationships have always been problematic at best. Truly happy long-lasting relationships are mystical events that occurred in the distant past or between people who settled down very late in life. How many people want to wait until they're 65 years and up for a last-ditch chance at relationship happiness? Can we ever get to a place of contentment, loving each other without the entire she said/ he said melodrama?

What do the experts say?

I've listened and studied a multitude of relationship experts over the course of my lifetime, from Dr. Amen, to Dr. Phil, from Ann Landers, to Dr. Tart, from Cosmo, to Essence Magazine. Thousands of published works by Psychologists and Psychiatrists, and literally countless other factions and facsimiles thereof, and no one tends to share concrete solutions for relationship problems. Well Philosopher 'X' is going to change that fact right now.

Common Answers and Theories for Relationship Problems or Success in Society Explained to you by the World's Greatest Relationshipologist (Relationshipologist is My New Created Scientific Word) ☺

- Remain celibate until you're married. In history, holy leaders and politicians have made of this age-old notion of not having intimacy until you are married a viable relationship choice; it's not very realistic. If you don't believe me consult your parent or parents about their past carnal intimate relations.

- Let your family and friends set you up with someone because they can vouch for the person's intentions. Matchmaking by peers can be problematic.

- Mental problems due to poor diets or direct head trauma can be identified via a brain scan. A Brain Spec Scan is used by medical specialists to locate areas of low electrical activity in your brain that can cause negative thoughts and behaviors. The brain scan is done so you can be advised on how to treat your targeted mental problems areas with nutrition, natural herbal remedies, and/or medicinal drugs. I like this because I believe our diets affect us in ways we've not yet discovered. Brain Spec Scanning is a costly process and most insurance plans do not cover it. Darn it Insurance!

• Seeking professional intermediary counseling from a knowledgeable relationship specialist, (i.e. Psychologist or Psychiatrist). Many relationship therapists whom themselves have gazed into the abyss of their own doomed relationships will attempt to help you to weather your relationship storm. Again, this can be a costly practice with no guarantee that it'll produce the blissful results you seek, but it may work for you. Get References.

Once, not long ago, I was invited to a paid dinner gathering of a panel of relationship experts consisting of men and women loaded with MD's and PHD's, (top notch college degrees). There was a large audience present with most the attending audience consisting of women and a few men. Many common problem solving techniques were mentioned by the Doctors and copies of their books on relationships swore to contain the essential keys to eternal matrimonial happiness. It was virtually guaranteed that these tools in their books would cure all the budding audience's relationship woes and have Mr. or Ms. Right knocking down the door to get to you! Many bought the advice but some of the audience didn't because the offered advice seemed stale and unrealistic which created more confusion about what was required to have a successful committed relationship.

Being a Philosopher and frustrated with hearing the same lame relationship remedies and theories I raised my hand to ask the highly educated and esteemed panel of experts a question; "Do you think that the problem with relationships today is that men are too callous and women are too smart?" I heard the jaws dropping in the convention hall as the panelists of relationship experts looked as though they wanted to crawl into a dark hole and hide. I truly wanted to know the answer. Gradually, a bloodcurdling hiss arose from the audience and before I was stoned, I asked to have a chance to explain myself. I admit that the crowd's reaction made me feel a bit uneasy, but I summoned the courage to continue the dialog. I quickly talked about my true family history of my Granddad and the uncle I never knew existed.

Also, I spoke about how unfavorable behavior by men in the past towards women was unequal and restricting to women's freedoms. How throughout history abusive men were reluctantly tolerated as a necessary evil by people who feared that speaking out about men's unfaithfulness might cause them harm and how in the past, women needed and depended on men more for their survival due to the circumstances of the ancient times they found themselves in. I then stated "Now, in modern times, it's different because the women in the past that may have needed a man to survive within a primitive and hostile environment, no longer needed men for their survival because the women of today are educated and financially capable of caring for themselves." That was the reason why I asked the Doctors on the panel that question. "Oh", replied the audience…

Many of the women in the audience proclaimed, "That's right, we don't have to take that kind of treatment anymore!" The men in the audience were quiet and to my dismay so were the Doctors and Psychologists on the relationship panel. With the question "Are men too callous and women too smart?" I effectively shut down the entire relationship forum, even though that wasn't my intention. Hence the name of this book, my quest to find and distribute honest answers and solutions about relationship issues, and hopes of helping human beings, (including myself), once and for all to honestly engage the *tuff* questions about relationships with integrity and candor.

By addressing the real problems in peoples' relationships, I want to clear up a lot of the world's troubles in the process. I know that's a tall order, but I consider myself the eternal optimist. If you think the reading has been rocky before, "then wait until you get a load of this!"

AT LAST - THE [REAL] TRUTH REVEALED

TRUTH#1 - When it comes to desired actions, desired outcomes, desired impressions, and the hopes of success in relationships, the bulk of humanity are - habitual chronic liars. True!

Need examples: I only have eyes for you...

Out of the thousands of men I've known from the young to the elderly, married or single, gay or straight, they all lie to their partners about their desire to be intimate with others 99% of the time. They'd willingly act on the urges if not for the undesired consequences including possible break-ups, not seeing their kids, monetary loss, ruining their reputations, ruining their careers, and hurting loved one's feelings.

However, if repressed physical urges are strong enough they interfere with the integrity of the survival program causing men to feel as though they are dying inside. Yikes! Thus, men feel that they must react or face the constant arousal torture echoing inside their minds. Picture a cigarette smoker who hasn't smoked in days but his best buddy walks by and blows cigarette smoke in his face - (the cigarette metaphorically means a hot female body). If the repressed urges are at their peak, a high percentage will smoke that unhealthy cigarette, even knowing it'll probably kill them or get them a hard slap on the face.

Once it was assumed I was asleep when I overheard through the thin walls of my home a close female relative talking to another close female family member in confidence, not meant for any man to hear. Both ladies stated that they've never known any woman to be completely faithful to a man, married or not, during their entire lives. Being a man I found it quite shocking that women enjoyed escapades as readily as men. I knew if I asked my female family members about what they just said about women being unfaithful, they'd likely evade the question and become very angry with me for eavesdropping on their private conversation. I didn't dare question them about this sensitive matter.

Women usually don't wish to be branded romantically adventurous in our double standard societies as it might lower their reputation and societal value. Listening with my then egotistical male ears, it seemed unbelievable to me that what I heard about feminine dalliances was true. My male mind needed further proof to validate this very interesting story. It took some years of research to locate the following scientific information, but here it is people:

Infidelity Dissected: Research on Why People Cheat

People with avoidant attachment styles are individuals uncomfortable with intimacy. They seem to be more inclined to have multiple intimacy encounters and cheat.

Source: Science Daily

The probability of someone cheating during the course of a relationship varies between 40 and 76 percent. "It's very high," says Geneviève Beaulieu-Pelletier, PhD student at the Université de Montréal's Department of Psychology.

"These numbers indicate that even if we get married with the best of intentions things don't always turn out the way we plan. What interests me about infidelity is why people are willing to conduct themselves in ways that could be very damaging to them and their relationship." The student wanted to know if the type of commitment a person has with his or her loved ones is correlated to the desire of having extra-marital affairs. "The emotional attachment we have with others is modeled on the type of parenting received during childhood," she says.

According to psychologists, people with avoidant attachment styles are individuals uncomfortable with intimacy and are therefore more likely to multiply intimacy encounters and cheat. But this has never been proved scientifically, which is what Beaulieu-Pelletier attempted to do in a series of four studies. The first study was conducted on 145 students with an average age of 23. Some 68 percent had thought about cheating and 41 percent had actually cheated. Intimacy satisfaction aside, the results indicated a strong correlation between infidelity and people with an avoidant attachment style.

The second study was conducted on 270 adults with an average age of 27. About 54 percent had thought about cheating and 39 percent had actually cheated. But the correlation is the same: people with an avoidant attachment style are more likely to cheat. "Infidelity could be a regulatory emotional strategy used by people with an avoidant attachment style. The act of cheating helps them avoid commitment phobia, distances them from their partner, and helps them keep their space and freedom."

Both these studies were followed up by two other studies that asked about the motives for infidelity. <u>The will to distance themselves from commitment and their partner</u> was the number one reason cited. These studies revealed no differences between men and women. Just as many men and women had an avoidant attachment style and the correlation with infidelity is just as strong on both sides. "Contrary to popular belief, infidelity isn't more prevalent in men," she says.

TRUTH#2 – People are total control freaks! True!

We want to control everything in our personal world and force our relationships to go our way even if it selfishly or unfairly limits the quality of life for our loved ones. This is Tyranny!

For the record: Not even God has the audacity to try to control you! God allows total anonymity to all living things, especially people! Yet people constantly try to do what the Creator of all things does not even do itself. Control People. Are you so much greater or wiser than God that you know the best direction for everyone you meet? Does everyone have to project your personal ideologies on what makes people self-expressed and happy? Maybe the less controlling you are - the Godlier you are.

I don't mean it's wrong to feel occasionally frustrated with your mate hanging out with the boys or girls too much. We all want and need quality time with our mates. I'm talking about controlling loved ones in other ways that tend to be unreasonable and cruel such as:

Always seeking to find a mental button to constantly push on your mate knowing that it will incite a negative response. People instinctively know that by pressing temperament buttons like* bad past issues, constant nagging about the way their mate looks, * possessing a current state of not having enough financial ambition, * pointing out perceived visible shortcomings daily, * overly jealous and oftentimes unfounded infidelity accusations, * deceptive and manipulated mind-games (sending mixed messages like I like or don't like that), * and general emotional, verbal, and physical abuse. That's not cool.

Other Ways People Control Other People

Withholding Intimacy: When there's no ailing physical or psychological reason for withholding intimacy from your committed mate, doing so willfully causes your life-partner insufferable and irritating grief. That's tantamount to abuse. This goes for men and women. It's a well-known implied fact of life, that when you start an intimately committed relationship with each other that you both agree to assist each other in the matters of carnal knowledge. Starving out your partner intimately for a no-good reason is physically and emotionally abusive.

Interesting Fact: The American-based Christian sect known as the Shakers (because of the way they convulse and tremble during church services). Their religious doctrine teaches them that having any intimate relations within your marriage is a sin and is forbidden. So, the Shakers adopt children to continue the families. Hmm…

Forcing Intimacy: When someone is forced into intimacy that's horrible because that's the crime of rape. No level of commitment justifies that type of abusive behavior. When you take your vows of marriage, spiritual commitment, or intimate commitment, even though you may want the relationship to last forever you didn't announce" I agree to stand by you through <u>unfair spirit-crippling abuse,</u> until death do us part." Never force yourself on someone. It's evil and can land you in prison for a long, long, long time. So, good people, to willingly endure abuse, with no perceived end in sight, is a sin of immense proportions. It's a sin that goes against the Creator, humanity, your family, and most importantly yourself.

I don't believe such spectacularly beautiful spiritual beings like yourselves were placed here to live and endure meaningless abuse from anyone. No, you were not. You are here to evolve spiritually and become your greatest version and be HAPPY. ☐

TRUTH#3 – Love is forever and you can only love one person at any given time. False!

Love, like any other feeling or emotion, it comes and goes because it's generated electrochemically in the brain. In relationships, when you're having negative emotions your love chemical potion isn't circulating in your brain very well, but it usually comes back when you calm down and forgive the transgression that caused your loving feeling to stop in the first place. Yes, you can love more than one significant other at the same time. This tends to become a very problematic issue because the question arises, "How can my mate love someone else when they are in love with me?!" How intolerable and disrespectful!

Perhaps your philandering mate never gave you the chance to converse on how to meet their intimate needs better? If he or she had given you the opportunity to show that you're more than capable of meeting each other's needs maybe things could and would be different? Sometimes infidelity can create communication that wasn't there previously and through forgiveness and counseling the couple reconnects and becomes more appreciative of each other than they ever did before.

If you feel an emotional disconnection developing within your relationship, the sooner you can introduce civil cooperative communication with each other, the better. That way you can work out the important issues causing problems in your relationship before they become unbearable. Communication is key if you wish to have a meaningful and loving relationship. Talk to each other!

IMPORTANT NOTE: When communicating with someone always attempt to keep the conversation civilized. Take a moment to ask yourself: Is my verbal dialogue Kind, Necessary, and True?

If the answer is no, then you're probably heading into troubled waters. Be ready to face the consequences that are bound to happen because of your foul, bad-mouthed uncivilized talk. Disrespectful demeaning speech can kill a relationship quick, fast, and in a hurry!

TRUTH#4 – Women do not enjoy intimacy as much as men. False!

Women have three to four times more pleasurable nerve endings in their happy place than men. Women can achieve multiple arrivals during intimacy sessions and everyone likes feeling good. But because ladies give birth to babies they usually take the moral high ground and limit their approach to acquiring intimacy. In other words, women tend to be more cautious in the intimacy area to avoid unwanted outcomes that are exclusively feminine based.

TRUTH#5 – Men would take a magic pill if it would get rid of bad physical urges. True!

I have spoken to many single, married, and divorced men and I asked them, "If it would ensure you'd never cheat on your loved one, would you be willing to take a pill that didn't physically harm you in any way, but would ensure that you remained satisfied with the lady you love, and that pill took away any desire you had to stray, would you take the pill?" One hundred percent of the men surveyed said YES! Men in most cases sincerely love the women they're willing to spend their lives with. It's just that the intimacy urges embedded in the DNA-genes are very powerful and hard to fight off. If scientists introduced this magic libido reduction pill men would take it and never stray again. Ladies, all your troubles with philandering men would be caput with your men taking the magic pill. So, Ladies get in the science lab and make it happen! I 've yet to ask a woman the magic pill question, so ladies feel free to inform me if you think women need a magic pill to keep them faithful.

TRUTH#6 – People may lose Physical Attraction with their partner as time goes on. True!

It's a sad fact of living life, that as we mature, our hair grays, body parts slide towards the south, frames grow plump and wide, skin spots and wrinkles appear on faces and hands, hair grows on areas of our bodies that we wish they didn't, and our teeth often find another place to live - besides in our mouths, like moving to a liquid filled glass on the bedside table. Yikes!

Aging can be a tough proposition but ideally, we hope we can love each other long enough and hard enough to overcome these physical changes that we'll encounter within the life of our relationships. So, true love can keep the fires of passion burning in our aging relationships, until we pass on to glory.   People tend to let themselves go physically when they've been in a committed relationship for extended periods of time. Why? Perhaps we get too comfortable and take our partners for granted. Thus, outward appearance changes may cause a lack of physical attraction with your mate and could affect the quality of your intimate relationship. This difficult dilemma goes for men and women, and you can't force someone to be attracted to you when they're not. Health and looks do matter in a relationship and that's a fact.

People are generally ok with some weight gain and other minor body changes, but not 30 to 60 pounds! Learn how to eat better and exercise every now and then. Exercise does not to have to be a complicated production. Do a bit of exercise now and then and watch what you eat and you'll be intimately sought after even in your great grandparenting years. Remember youthful beauty fades away over time so replace it with the grandeur of mature beauty because it's been proven that people tend to enjoy their lives even more when they mature in age.

Consider "Minimum Dose Effective Exercise" – a complete workout in 10 minutes or less!

I personally like growing older and wiser. I hold a great deal of respect for those who have come before me and braved the worse to ensure that we humans have a chance to give living life a try. Do you know that it took the coupling of at least 1 million or more of your ancestors to get you here – alive now. Living, dying, and growing older is a life cycle we all must all go through. So, now that we're here; let's love each other and stop thinking it's better to be one age or the other. Enjoy your youthful age but cherish and respect your elders. Learn from them and if they're good teachers, allow them to learn from you as well. Visit with the elders from time to time, because one day they'll move on to the spirit plane and you will have lost a great bonding and learning opportunity from a person's lifetime of experience. Love your elders!

TRUTH#7 – All human relationships are experiments, only not in a clinical setting. True!

That's right we're all scientists, because the love experiment mixes different people together with different preferences, attitudes, personalities, beliefs, fears, emotions, resources, social statuses, habits, and hobbies. The outcome of a successful relationship is usually requiring us to reach the lifelong distinction of "till death do us part scenario." People often ask elderly couples what formula they used to stay married for so many long and blissful years. The answers given by the elderly couples seem to revolve around tolerance of one's mistakes, supporting each other through hard times and good times, exploring fun, new, and exciting things together, and never accepting that divorce is an option. Just Say No to Divorce. □

TRUTH#8 – When I say "I do" in a marriage ceremony it means that all the flaws in my relationship will be wiped away. False!

False! Marriage will test you in ways unimagined. No one is without some type of physical or emotional flaw no matter how much you love them or how grand your intentions. Just be as prepared as you possibly can by getting educated about each other and about how to create better relationships.

TRUTH#9 – African-Americans have the lowest marriage rate in the western hemisphere. True!

The rate of African-Americans not married in America versus married in other western countries varies but generally hovers around these numbers: African-Americans married 30 percent, and those unmarried 70 percent. There are many beautiful single-women parenting children on their own in America. Because of all the issues people have with relationships it's understandable that single-parenthood can bring about a plethora of problems such as:

- Lack of resources (i.e. food shortages, the expenses of daycare, quality time off to go out and enjoy life, dead-beat dads, etc.).

Problems revolving around single-parenthood has seemingly decimated the African-American communities in western countries, if you agree with the societal statistics. The weight of too many negative consequences from becoming a struggling single-parent can be very destructive to a mother and child - no matter what race you are, or what community you live in. Think very hard before you become a single-parent because you may create a scenario in which you and your loved ones may never positively recover.

TRUTH#10 – Single mothers are the angriest people in America. True!

Per a five-year scientific study looking to discover the angriest people in America and the causes of their anger, single mothers were number one on the angry list. The study cited the hardships of raising kids on their own and negative feelings of abandonment. Number two on the angriest people in America list were those with financial difficulties, oh and number three were teenagers. Teenagers – why so serious?

TRUTH#11 – Size matters! True & False!

In some cases, size, does matter. But, if you're a male with a smaller phallus and treat a person with confidence, care, love, and dignity in the intimacy department, you'll find that your partner will be quite satisfied. So, don't keep asking about it and enjoy! Why? Repetitive questioning rules out the 'C' in the confidence factor and actually it's estimated that less than 20 percent of women can accommodate large phalluses comfortably enough to make them want that, and that only. Ladies tend to prefer confident caring partners and not being uncomfortable when they're being intimate.

Where size really matters is the size of your bank account. As a famous chef said, "When poverty comes into the home, love goes out the window." Ideally, if anything matters it should be that someone will love you for you, just the way you are. Some women don't desire any physical contact of any kind with anyone. Some people chose to abstain and can live very satisfying and happy lives. Go figure.

For The Ladies: Most men don't care about big chests, they love you with or without large appendages. If you're in a relationship with a man who insists on you physically augmenting yourself to become beautiful, be careful. Men like that tend to be very shallow minded and want you more as a trophy than a caring, free-thinking partner. Think about it?

TRUTH#12 – Women love looking at pornography just as much as Men. True & False!

A scientific test using electrodes to measure arousal in men and women while watching pornography showed that both men and women were equally aroused by lude movies. The men overwhelmingly admitted to that fact in post-questioning interviews that they were aroused. Yet 100% of the women denied that they were aroused by looking at the lude acts. In other words, all the ladies politely lied! Sometimes women will admit to liking erotic books and movies like (50 Shades of Grey). Funny how the intimacy is never mentioned by the ladies as a reason for liking erotic books and movies. □

TRUTH#13 – Soul mates???

Call me a hopeless romantic but the great and powerful Philosopher 'X' chooses not to apply true or false to the soul mate possibility. I know I've been hard hitting with the contents in this book, but my hope that there is some love magic floating around in the world means I'm going easy on this one. On occasion, I speak to people who proudly proclaim, "At last I've found my soul mate!" and I am genuinely happy for them. I say, "God forbid if something happens and you lose that person in an accident, would you ever find it in your heart to love another person again, and if so would that person perhaps be your intended soul mate, or is it possible that you can have more than one soul mate in a lifetime?"

Ok I know that sounds pessimistic but I really do mean well. I'll leave this for the readers to decide.

TRUTH#14 – Masturbation is a virtue. True!

Why is masturbation a virtue? Repression fuels the fire of deviant behavior especially when it involves the libido. It's unnatural to try and stop the reproduction drive (aka libido), because it serves the purpose of getting you here and making sure you are not here by yourself. Repressing the human libido for any reason is dangerous!

For one thing, it can't be done completely unless you are brain damaged in a physical way. To attempt total libido repression creates a fertile mental breeding ground for perverted deviance to grow and manifest into victimizing innocent people - especially in men. These situations can often cause incredibly life-altering results, which can lead to physical and psychological abuses of young children which may cause them to become irreversibly damaged, both mentally and physically for a lifetime.

Commonly, intimacy repression with male and female adults creates situations within their minds of loneliness, confusion, irritability, rejection, and desperation. These feelings can lead to poor decisions, reckless liaisons, feeling intense feelings of guilt and shame, and feeling used once you've submitted to fulfill your biological urges with someone who doesn't care about you - at all. Intimacy Repression can cause unwanted pregnancies and can also cause people to become more susceptible to physical and emotional abuse. Why? The blinding effect of swirling arousal emotions storming in your body can mentally make you toss helpful intimacy caution out of the window.

I asked many single mothers and fathers if they planned to create a baby so they could provide a beautiful life for their bundle of joy. 9 times out of 10 the pregnancy was an accident. A very close lady friend told me once that she'd been in a few unsuccessful relationships in which she felt pressured into having relations without the exclusive relationship commitment she desired. Because she felt used for her body she decided that taking a celibacy break was warranted and that break lasted well over a year.

She said, for reasons she couldn't explain, she began to have odd romantic fantasies during the day and weird lucid romantic dreams that woke her up during the night! This caused her much emotional unease and it was terribly out of her character to have such offensive arousing thoughts. She even felt she might submit to the same non-committal type of man again which would be bringing her right back to square-one of feeling used. The lady was a former girlfriend of mine and I felt a great deal of empathy for her and her plight.

I asked her if she had ever masturbated during her celibacy and she said, "No I don't think it's right to do that!" She was a very religious person by the way. Over the years, I've heard similar stories of smoldering mental turmoil from men and women who became celibate to honor their relationship principles. How ironic that we find fault in the very desires the Creator has bestowed upon us, as if they were not to be understood and used with kindness, reverence, and care. It may sound counter-intuitive but masturbation can ease the burning physical urges a great deal and tends to make people more relaxed and calm. Masturbation puts people in tune with their bodies and can help people make better relationship choices because they're not feeling over anxious. Also, scientifically masturbation reduces the chances of men developing prostate cancer.

So, Ladies and Gents, if you chose to pleasure yourselves be safe and don't go overboard. As too much of a good thing can be just as bad as not enough. Oh, people if your perspective other takes care of themselves sometimes - even if they're in a relationship with you – don't beat them up about it. Sometimes even life-mates need private quality time. ☺

TRUTH#15 – Money destroys relationships. True & False!

If you review the top ten reasons why relationships fail, money is usually in the top three items on the list. Oftentimes money problems make it to number one! Even obtaining a higher list position than the dreaded act of promiscuous infidelity. Why can money tear us apart so easily, where angels fear to tread? Scientific researchers speculate it's because both parents must work long hours away from each other and their children to earn enough funds to pay bills, (i.e. utilities, rent or mortgage, transportation, food, medicine, etc....).

This fact tends to place severe strains and stresses on the closeness of the family unit. The familial setting tends to erode very badly when there's not enough money to provide for a stable family lifestyle. So, it's a <u>lack of money</u> that creates scarcity that can greatly limit the quality time desperately needed to have peace in today's households. Lack of money can greatly limit the availability of essential resources that's a major reason a lot of evil scenarios can occur at home because parenting adults are unable to be home to supervise the family activity. People simply don't have the time to get to know each other anymore and are too tired and overworked to respond wholeheartedly the way they would like to with their loved ones.

As a therapist, I've personally noticed a lot of men and women being married to their job, meaning their job commands precedence over family activities. This is always problematic especially when children are involved. Also, I've seen the mortality in birth rates rise significantly because women are working too hard in high-pressure jobs. We must find a way to provide for women when they're expecting a baby. The European country of France treats their expecting mothers' well by giving them paid leave from working on their job so that they can have successful stress-free pregnancies. To see how stress affects female mammalian reproduction, research the mating habits of the African Mole-Rat Colonies. Yes, there's a human social correlation…look it up.

FACT: Over 90 percent of crimes in this World are committed over money!

For possible alternate solutions to the money issue, other than winning the lottery, working on a job that requires very little time, or marrying a rich person; go to: www.thevenusproject.com

Speaking of marrying a rich person, why do you suppose that approximately 90 percent of rich people, who are already rich, marry other rich people? I admit this percentage is an educated guess. It's a no-brainer why a poor person would want to marry into money – for the money! Sometimes it may be because of love? Rich people marry each other, because like everyone else they wish to extend and enhance their positions in life to ensure survivability. Meaning that even if they have enough money to last ten generations they still want more. The rich simply don't wish to look beyond their diamond encrusted life-box to even contemplate that a poor person with integrity can enrich their lives. Is love involved in their decision when they marry their rich human counterpart (aka a walking-talking Federal Reserve)? Who knows? Guess you'll just have to ask a rich person if you're curious.

When it comes to the Almighty Dollar, Peso, Yen, Baht, Ruble, Rupee or Euro, (depending on where you live), one of the biggest complaints from men about women is that even if a man is a nice guy, women seem to constantly choose to pass them up in a mad pursuit to pen down the million-dollar man. Many men claim "I'm hard working, ambitious, decent looking, take care of my health, and I have honorable intentions, but I'm not given a chance because - I'm not rich!" Ladies, sometimes it makes for a better love story when you help each other to the top rather than being a slave to big money and loving an unappreciative rich man. I'm just saying…

Truth#16 – it's ok to look at other people. True!

Beautiful people in all shapes and sizes live in this world and it's nothing wrong with looking at them (briefly), if you're out with your man or woman in public. People are living breathing works of art and to restrict people from looking at them because of jealousy is abusive, foolish, and immature. So, stop starting fights over looking at someone, it's disruptive, childish, and stupid.

TRUTH#17 – The 300 Spartans that died in the legendary Battle of Thermopylae, made famous by the movie 300, were most likely, all practicing homosexuals. True!

The Spartan Empire was the most powerful and elite fighting force in ancient Greece. It was mandated by compulsory custom in the City of Sparta that their young pre-teen male warriors were partnered with mature male soldiers to learn the ways of warfare and love. Part of the logic behind this is that if a man truly loves the person fighting by his side, he would fight much more aggressively to valiantly protect them. Even if that meant dying to save them in battle. Because the warriors loved each other so much a new law had to be passed in Sparta stating that Spartan Warriors for the greater glory of the republic, in order to gain social status and rank, and remain a Spartan Citizen, you must marry and have children with a Spartan woman. That's right the guys stopped messing with the girls so the government had to step in.

Note: *Most laws are mankind's way of attempting to prevent a problem from happening or recurring by attaching penalties and punishment to those who would break those laws.*

During most of the reign of the Greek and Roman Empires the definition of true love was homosexual love. This premise of same gender love was also well received in Asian and Native American cultures. But why not now?

In short homosexuality was never a big deal in the western world until the creation of the Catholic controlled Holy Roman Empire, and the different Christian offshoot sects that followed. Homosexuality is also practiced by a large percentage of the mammalian animal kingdom from apes to zebras. The truth of the matter is that homosexuality has been around in other animals before mankind even existed. Many scientists have discovered that homosexuality is largely due to people being born with certain types of genetic traits that cause them to be attracted to the same gender and is beyond their mental control.

Why is this important and what does this have to do with relationships?

Many men and women, married or unmarried, are closeted homosexuals. Some gay people can intentionally keep their lifestyle relatively secret from their friends, partners, and family members in the hopes that secrecy will protect them from social embarrassment or rejection. But sometimes the cat is let out of the bag and the secret life of a person involved in same-gender love is discovered. Oftentimes causing a huge scandal which destroys the persons' life and affects their families. If I were to tell you about the sports athletes, celebrities, holy men and women, and local and federal government officials that participate in clandestine same-gender escapades you'd begin to think that perhaps homosexuals were in the majority of society and not the minority.

Due to the harsh treatment, prominent gay people would suffer from if they were discovered, they tend to keep their tastes hidden to avoid unwanted persecution and repercussions. Even if it means keeping their secret lifestyle hid from their families. Some gay people will attempt to throw people off their trail by publicly condemning other homosexuals in the hopes that their love-life won't be discovered. Oh, the hypocrisy of it all. Remember the scientific tests in **TRUTH#4** about women denying that they were aroused by pornography? Well the same scientist tested men to see if they would be aroused by male-on-male pornography.

The researchers found that the men who were claiming they were straight heterosexuals and protested very harshly about the evils of homosexuality and adamantly criticized homosexuals, denied being physically aroused by homosexual porn. But, the protesting males gained certain heights, so to speak, which they also denied having achieved. Heights like that in men can only happen with an aroused libido. The evidence of arousal was scientifically indisputable because electrodes that were specifically designed to detect male arousal was attached to their private areas that amply displayed that men were indeed aroused by the male on male pornography. Whereas, men that claimed they were straight heterosexuals that had no problems with homophobia, (hate or disdain for gay people), and held no ill will towards gay people, did not receive arousal through viewing the gay porn. The heterosexual men who vehemently protested the gay lifestyle seemed to have all the characteristics of closeted homosexuals.

Unfortunately, we live in a world of lies and contradictions and because of that fact we set ourselves up for lives filled with harmful deceits. Deceits that often don't show up until many lives are embroiled in a volatile mix of secrets and betrayals. Will modern-day people ever become willing and brave enough to go beyond the impossible emotional and physical restrictions we place on ourselves? Renowned psychologist Dr. Drew stated, "True straight men don't get aroused at all by male porn. So, if you want to know if your man's gay, watch some gay porn with him. See if he gets a rise out of the deal, or not?" (Paraphrased but close to what he said). Many therapists believe that physical attraction and arousal can have a sliding-scale changing from, straight to bi, or bi to gay. Switches of preference can happen at different times in a person's life, especially women, whom for some reason can transition intimately on a sliding-scale easier than men. Anyway, we need to become more compassionate and understanding with each other in matters of the heart.

TRUTH#18 – Teaching children intimacy education greatly lessens the risk of them having unwanted pregnancies, abortions, and STD's, (Intimate Transmitted Diseases). True!

What does teaching intimacy education have to do with having a great relationship? Because when your child suffers, you suffer! People that love you suffer, when you suffer! Especially your parents. You're always your parents Baby. ☺ Studies and statistics from progressive western countries around the world (particularly in Europe), show that the earlier you teach responsible intimacy education to children (in a school environment), that the children being taught have way fewer problems in the complicated arena of intimacy relationships.

Make sure you responsibly educate your child (if you are blessed with one), so they're aware of the ups and downs, and dangers, of certain relations. So, that the child will be responsible, well-informed, and protected from potential predators and would-be suitors. The children need to know vital intimacy information and they will appreciate your honesty, knowledge, and candor for the duration of their lives.

FYI: Child Sex Education Info 101 – (Parental Guidance Is Suggested)

SOURCE: The National Child Traumatic Stress Network - www.NCTSN.org

Sexual Development and Behavior in Children

Your five-year-old daughter is playing in her room with a couple of friends. You hear a lot of giggling and squealing. When you open the door to check on the kids, you find them sitting on the floor with their panties off, pointing at and touching each other's genitals. What do you do? Every day, parents around the world are faced with situations like this. Being caught off-guard by young children's self-exploration and curiosity about body parts and sexual issues is one of the uncomfortable realities of parenting, and can raise a host of troubling questions, such as, "Is my child normal?" or "Should I be worried?" or "What should I say?"

Although talking with children about bodily changes and sexual matters may feel awkward, providing children with accurate, age-appropriate information is one of the most important things parents can do to make sure children grow up safe, healthy, and secure in their bodies. Sexual development and behavior in young children: The basics, like all forms of human development and sexual development begins at birth. Sexual development includes not only the physical changes that occur as children grow, but also the sexual knowledge and beliefs they come to

85

learn and the behaviors they show. Any given child's sexual knowledge and behavior is strongly influenced by:

The child's age 1-3, what the child observes (including the sexual behaviors of family and friends). Age 4, what the child is taught (including cultural and religious beliefs concerning sexuality and physical boundaries). "Young people do not wake up on their thirteenth birthday, somehow transformed into a sexual being overnight. Even young children are sexual in some form."

Very young and preschool-aged children (four or younger) are naturally immodest, and may display open— and occasionally startling--curiosity about other people's bodies and bodily functions, such as touching women's breasts, or wanting to watch when grownups go to the bathroom. Wanting to be naked (even if others are not) and showing or touching private parts while in public are also common in young children. They are curious about their own bodies and may quickly discover that touching certain body parts feels nice. (For more on what children typically do at this and other ages, see Table 1.)

As children age and interact more with other children (approximately ages 4–6), they become more aware of the differences between boys and girls, and more social in their exploration. In addition to exploring their own bodies through touching or rubbing their private parts (masturbation), they may begin "playing doctor" and copying adult behaviors such as kissing and holding hands. As children become increasingly aware of the social rules governing sexual behavior and language (such as the importance of modesty or which words are considered "naughty"), they may try to test these rules by using naughty words. They may also ask more questions about sexual matters, such as where babies come from, and why boys and girls are physically different.

Table 1: Common Sexual Behaviors in Childhood1, 3, 6 Age Uncommon/Problematic Behaviors

Preschool children (less than 4 years)

Exploring and touching private parts, in public and in private ■ Rubbing private parts (with hand or against objects) ■ Showing private parts to others ■ Trying to touch mother's or other Women's breasts ■ Removing clothes and wanting to be naked ■ Attempting to see other people when they are naked or undressing (such as in the bathroom) Asking questions about their own—and others'—bodies and bodily functions ■ Talking to children their own age about bodily functions such as "poop" and "pee".

Young Children (approximately 4-6 years)

Purposefully touching private parts (masturbation), occasionally in the presence of others ■ Attempting to see other people when they are naked or undressing ■ Mimicking dating behavior (such as kissing, or holding hands) Talking about private parts and using "naughty" words, even when they don't understand the meaning Exploring private parts with children their own age (such as "playing doctor", "I'll show you mine if you show me yours," etc.)

School-Aged Children (approximately 7-12 years)

Purposefully touching private parts (masturbation), usually in private ■ Playing games with children their own age that involve sexual behavior (such as "truth or dare", "playing family," or "boyfriend/girlfriend") Attempting to see other people naked or undressing ■ Looking at pictures of naked or partially naked people ■ Viewing/listening to sexual content in media (television, movies, games, the Internet, music, etc.) Wanting more privacy (for example, not wanting to undress in front of other people) and being reluctant to talk to adults about sexual issues; Beginnings of sexual attraction to/interest in peers.

Once children enter grade school (approximately ages 7–12), their awareness of social rules increases and they become more modest and want more privacy, particularly around adults. Although self-touch (masturbation) and sexual play continue, children at this age are likely to hide these activities from adults. Curiosity about adult sexual behavior increases—particularly as puberty approaches—and children may begin to seek out sexual content in television, movies, and printed material. Telling jokes and "dirty" stories is common. Children approaching puberty are likely to start displaying romantic and sexual interest in their peers. (For more, see Table 1.)

Although parents often become concerned when a child shows sexual behavior, such as touching another child's private parts, these behaviors are not uncommon in developing children. Most sexual play is an expression of children's natural curiosity and should not be a cause for concern or alarm. In general, "typical" childhood sexual play and exploration: Occurs between children who play together regularly and know each other well ■ Occurs between children of the same general age and physical size ■ Is spontaneous and unplanned ■ Is infrequent ■ Is voluntary (the children agreed to the behavior, none of the involved children seem uncomfortable or upset) Is easily diverted when parents tell children to stop and explain privacy rules.

Some childhood sexual behaviors indicate more than harmless curiosity, and are considered sexual behavior problems. Sexual behavior problems may pose a risk to the safety and well-being of the child and other children. Sexual behavior problems include any act that: Is clearly beyond the child's developmental stage (for example, a three-year-old attempting to kiss an adult's genitals) Involves threats, force, or aggression ■ Involves children of widely different ages or abilities (such as a 12-year-old "playing doctor" with a four-year-old) Provokes strong emotional reactions in the child—such as anger or anxiety.

Responding to Sexual Behaviors

Situations like the one described at the beginning of this handout can be unsettling for parents. However, these situations also offer excellent opportunities to assess how much children understand and to teach important information about sexual matters.

The first step is to try to figure out what actually happened. To do this, it's important to stay calm. Staying calm will allow you to make clear decisions about what you say and/or do, rather than acting on strong emotions.

Coping with your own reactions to remain composed, try taking a long, deep breath, counting to ten, or even closing the door and stepping away for a couple of minutes before saying anything. In the case described above, a parent might calmly tell the children that it's time to get dressed and then ask each child to go to a different room in the house. After taking a few moments to collect his or her thoughts—and to consult with a spouse or partner if feeling very unsettled— the parent could then talk to each child one-on-one. When talking to children about sexual behaviors, it's important to maintain a calm and even tone of voice and to ask open-ended questions as much as possible, so the children can tell what happened in their own words, rather than just answering yes or no. So, in this case, a parent might ask each child:

What were you doing? ■ How did you get the idea? ■ How did you learn about this? ■ How did you feel about doing it?

In the opening scenario, all of the children involved were about the same age, had been playmates for some time, and seemed to be enjoying their game. So, it's likely the children were just curious and playing around and that no one was upset about what happened. If you encounter a situation where the children are a little embarrassed but otherwise not distressed, this can present an ideal opportunity for teaching the children about healthy boundaries and rules about sexual behavior.

Educating Children about Sexual Issues

Just because a behavior is typical doesn't mean the behavior should be ignored. Often, when children participate in sexual behavior it indicates that they need to learn something. Teach what the child needs to know, given the situation. In this case, for example, the parent might teach the children that it's okay to be curious about other people's bodies, but that private parts should be kept private, even with friends.

Although children usually respond well when parents take the time to give them correct information and answer their questions, it is important to provide information that is appropriate to the child's age and developmental level.

In Table 2, you will find an overview of some of the most important information and safety messages for children of various ages. Keep in mind that you do not need to bombard children with information all at once. Let the situation, and the child's questions, guide the lessons you share. The important thing is to let children know that you are ready to listen and to answer whatever questions they may have.

Too often, children get the majority of their sexual education from other children and from media sources such as television shows, songs, movies, and video games. Not only is this information often wrong, it may have very little to do with sexual values that parents want to convey. Explicit adult sexual activities are sometimes found during "family time" television shows, in commercials, and on cartoon/children's channels, and can have an influence on children's behaviors.

Controlling media exposure and providing appropriate alternatives is an important part of teaching children about sexual issues. Get to know the rating systems of games, movies, and television shows and make use of the parental controls available through many internet, cable, and satellite providers.

Myth: Talking about sex with my children will just encourage them to become sexually active. Fact: In a recent survey of American teens, 9 out of 10 teens said it would be easier to delay sexual activity and prevent unwanted pregnancy if they were able to have "more open, honest conversations" with their parents on these topics. When you talk honestly with your children about sexual issues, you can give them the knowledge and skills they need to keep safe and to make good decisions about relationships and intimacy.

However, don't assume that just by activating those controls you will be taking care of the situation. It's very important for you to be aware of what your children are watching on television and online, and make time to watch television with them. When appropriate, you can use this time as a springboard to talk about sexual or relationship issues, and to help children develop the skills to make healthy decisions about their behavior and relationships.

Table 2: What to Teach Preschool children (less than 4 years)

Basic Information, boys and girls are different ■ Accurate names for body parts of boys and girls ■ Babies come from mommies ■ Rules about personal boundaries (for example, keeping private parts covered, not touching other children's private parts) Give simple answers to all questions about the body and bodily functions.

Safety Information The difference between "okay" touches (which are comforting, pleasant, and welcome) and "not okay" touches (which are intrusive, uncomfortable, unwanted, or painful) Your body belongs to you ■ Everyone has the right to say "no" to being touched, even by grownups. No one—child or adult--has the right to touch your private parts ■ It's okay to say "no" when grownups ask you to do things that are wrong, such as touching private parts or keeping secrets from mommy or daddy. There is a difference between a "surprise" --which is something that will be revealed sometime soon, like a present, and a "secret," which is something you're never supposed to tell. Stress that it is never okay to keep secrets from mommy and daddy, who to tell if people do "not okay" things to you, or ask you to do "not okay" things to them.

Young Children (approximately 4-6 years)

Basic Information: Boys' and girls' bodies change when they get older. ■ Simple explanations of how babies grow in their mothers' wombs and about the birth process. Rules about personal boundaries (such as, keeping private parts covered, not touching other children's private parts) Simple answers to all questions about the body and bodily functions. Touching your own private parts can feel nice, but is something done in private

Safety Information: Sexual abuse is when someone touches your private parts or asks you to touch their private parts; It is sexual abuse even if it is by someone you know ■ Sexual abuse is NEVER the child's fault ■ If a stranger tries to get you to go with him or her, run and tell a parent, teacher, neighbor, police officer, or other trusted adult; Who to tell if people do "not okay" things to you, or ask you to do "not okay" things to them.

School-Aged Children (approximately 7-12 years)

Basic Information: What to expect and how to cope with the changes of puberty (including menstruation and wet dreams). Basics of reproduction, pregnancy, and childbirth ■ Risks of sexual activity (pregnancy, sexually transmitted diseases). Basics of contraception ■ Masturbation is common and not associated with long term problems, but should be done in private.

Safety Information: Sexual abuse may or may not involve touch ■ How to maintain safety and personal boundaries when chatting or meeting people online. How to recognize and avoid risky social situations ■ Dating rules ■

Parents play a pivotal role in helping their children develop healthy attitudes and behaviors towards sexuality. Although talking with your children about sex may feel outside your comfort zone, there are many resources available to help you begin and continue the conversation about sexuality. Providing close supervision, and providing clear, positive messages about modesty, boundaries and privacy are crucial as children move through the stages of childhood. By talking openly with your children about relationships, intimacy, and sexuality, you can foster their healthy growth and development.

TRUTH#19 – Grown-ups need intimacy education too. True!

Women, you need to take the lead with educating your male partners on how to best serve your emotional and physical needs by telling men what you want and like during intimacy. Ladies, if you're new to the intimacy department there's no shame in letting your partner know that fact so that you both can explore and discover what you want and like together. Ladies, consider the male to be an uneducated mechanical apparatus' that has to follow your lead to create a fulfilling intimate life with you. Don't be spiteful or demeaning to your partner when training him to fulfill your desires because men are more sensitive than they let on. I know it's a chore but training your partner can lead to many hours of blissful ecstasy.

Also, men don't expect your female partner to be a pornstar. That stuff on video is make-believe and not reality. So, be compassionate and respectful to the ladies and don't push too hard because you will be quickly kicked out of the relationship by a woman who's not into that sort of thing - real fast. Respect the Ladies!

TRUTH#20 – You are the reason you're in a bad relationship - not the other person. True!

It's time to take responsibility for your own choices! I repeat, "You must take responsibility for your own choices!" Especially with whom you're in a relationship with. If you have a problem with your partner's drug use, smoking, snoring, quickies, horror movies, the clothing on the floor, looking at other people, emotional and physical abuse, jealousy, money spent, etc…. can't you see the other person may be totally fine with the way they are? You're not ok with them! You! You have the problem with the way he or she is being and treating you in the relationship. That ultimately makes you responsible because you chose to stay in the bad relationship. So, if you can't reconcile the problems you have with your partner then you're the fool that's responsible for sticking around in an awful relationship? YOU!

Get out the home, cry, shout, or do whatever, and move on with your life. Life's too short for that sort of foolishness. Like Tammy and Millicent state in their - **LIGMO** - Life and Relationship Training Program. Let It Go, Move On! **(LIGMO)!**

One Way We Destroy Perfectly Good Relationships – Self-Fulfilling Prophecy

A Self-fulfilling prophecy is engaging in behaviors that obtain results that confirm your existing pre-conceived trouble-is-coming attitude. A self-fulfilling prophecy is a prediction that causes itself to become true. For example: I believe that I am going to do poorly in school, so I decrease the effort I put into my assignments and studying, and I end up doing poorly, just as I thought. Another common example is relationships; I think my relationship with my significant other is going to fail, so I start acting differently, pulling away emotionally.

Because of my actions, I actually cause my close relationships to fail. This is a powerful tool used by "psychics" – they implant an idea in your mind, and you eventually make it happen because you think it will.

Source: Top 10 Common Faults in Human Thought - Listverse.com

TRUTH#21 - You are the reason you're in a great relationship! True!

Being truly happy in your intimate relationship means you've learned how to weather the struggles of life and through it all you've gained meaningful life wisdom. You realize self-love (loving yourself), is the first key to becoming self-governing in your ability to put aside past baggage, so you can appropriately give and receive love in your relationships. Success in relationships shows to the world that you love yourself greatly and from that love you create more love with the people you care about, effortlessly. This abundance of self-love spills over into your mate, family, friends, and community.

Now isn't that a beautiful way to live? Great Relationships is the most important thing because to have a high-quality of life you need to be surrounded by people who love you and want you to be successful. People that have great relationships proudly do what's needed to preserve and serve their own best interests and their loved ones' best interests without being mistreated, or mistreating others. Great relationships encompass the

Poker Principle: *You must know when to hold em' and when to fold em'.* Be happy and chose your relationships wisely. You oversee the quality of the relationships you live in, so please choose wisely.

TRUTH#22 – Intimate Relations is the most important thing in a relationship? False!

Intimate physical relations are an important part of intimate relationships but overall it plays a very small role in the success of lasting relationships. At best, if you intimately indulge, "How many hours of the day do you participate in intimate physical activity?" 1 hour, 2, 3 hours? They're still 21 or more hours left in the day. Physical-based relationships usually don't last very long because love-sports can't continue 24 hours a day. So, if you chose to have a mate, be truthful and forthcoming from the very beginning of the initial stages of the relationship. I have learned from personal experience that honesty from the beginning is less stressful and less hurtful to you and your mate.

The truthful approach plays a more positive role in the relationships we participate in by affording each person to build a relationship on more stable grounds. Playing the game of telling him or her what they want to hear just so you can get whatever you want, will never create the peace of mind you wish to manifest in your life. It will create quite the opposite. Trouble! A lot of Trouble! Lying to manipulate someone creates hateful and vengeful consequences from your EX-mate that you don't want to have to deal with. Trust me!

Betrayal by lying deceit makes you look cheap and perverted in the eyes of your EX's, as well as other people in your life. It's tough to hold on to respect and maintain peace inside an environment of people that think you're a full-time jerk.

TRUTH#23 – Everybody Farts! True!   (Toot-Toot!)

That's right everybody farts! From the First Lady, to those incredibly beautiful Sports Illustrated Magazine models. Everybody, farts, burps, has an occasional runny nose, coughs, sneezes, urinates, and defecates (poops). Get Over It! We're all organic based life forms and that means we produce waste and gas, because we must eat and drink food to live. Stop being mean to each other and behaving so repulsed at something that everyone doesn't always have the ability to control.

Believe me if I never had to fart or burp again I wouldn't. Why? Because I hate the awful looks and mean comments that you get from loved ones and strangers when my biogas emissions erupt. But even book writers are human too. Lighten up for goodness sakes! I personally find it funny when my lady friends toot. Just roll down the window or spray some air freshener. ☺

FART FACTS: 10 Facts about Farting

SOURCE: Oddee.com

Why do we fart? Why do farts smell? Passing gas may be embarrassing for most of us, but it might make you feel better to know that it's one of the most common bodily functions of all time. Everyone does it, from Halle Berry to the Queen of England. In fact, the word "fart" is one of the oldest words in the English language! Read on to discover more fascinating facts about cutting the cheese.

1. What Is A Fart, Exactly?

Farts are caused by trapped air, which can come from many sources. Some of it is air that we have swallowed while chewing or drinking. Some air is caused by gas seeping into our intestines from our blood, and some gas is produced by chemical reactions in our intestines or bacteria living in our guts.

A typical fart is composed of about 59 percent nitrogen, 21 percent hydrogen, 9 percent carbon dioxide, 7 percent methane and 4 percent oxygen. Only about one percent of a fart contains hydrogen sulfide gas and mercaptans, which contain sulfur, and the sulfur is what makes farts stink.

Farts make a sound when they escape due to the vibrations of the rectum. The loudness may vary depending on how much pressure is behind the gas, as well as the tightness of the sphincter muscles.

2. Why Do Farts Smell Bad?

The more sulfur-rich your diet is, the more terrible your farts will smell. Some foods contain more sulfur than others, which is why eating things like beans, cabbage, cheese, soda, and eggs can cause gas that will peel the paint off the walls!

3. People Pass Gas About 14 Times Per Day

The average person produces about half a liter of farts every single day, and even though many women won't admit it, women do fart just as often as men. In fact, a study has proven that when men and women eat the exact same food, woman tend to have even more concentrated gas than men.

If a person were to fart continuously for 6 years and 9 months, they would produce gas with the equivalent energy of an atomic bomb.

4.   Farts Have Been Clocked At A Speed Of 10 Feet Per Second.

Though farts come out with varying velocities, we don't typically smell them for about 10-15 seconds after letting them rip. This is because it takes that long for the odor to reach your nostrils.

5.   Holding Farts In Could Be Bad For Your Health

Doctors disagree on whether or not holding in a fart is bad for your health. Some experts think that farts are a natural part of your digestive system, so holding them in won't harm you. Others think that at best, holding them in can cause gas, bloating, and other uncomfortable symptoms, and at worst, repressing gas can cause hemorrhoids or a distended bowel.

6.   For Some Cultures, Farting Is No Big Deal

While most cultures feel that farts should be suppressed in polite company, there are some cultures that not only don't mind letting them fly in public, but they actually enjoy it. An Indian tribe in South America called the Yanomami fart as a greeting, and in China you can actually get a job as a professional fart-smeller! In ancient Rome, Emperor Claudius, fearing that holding farts in was bad for the health, passed a law stating that it was acceptable to break wind at banquets.

7. Farts Are Flammable

As stated above, the methane and hydrogen in bacteria-produced farts make your gas highly flammable. This is why some people think it's a fun party trick to hold a lighter up to their bums and let one fly; doing so produces a big burst of flame, but is obviously very dangerous.

In rare cases, a build-up of flammable gasses in the intestines has caused explosions during intestinal surgeries!

8. Termites Produce The Most Farts Of Any Other Animal

It's hard to believe that the tiny termite is responsible for a great deal of our global warming problem on the planet. Termites fart more than any other animal, which produces methane gas. According to the Environmental Protection Agency, "Global emissions of methane due to termites are estimated to be between 2 and 22 TG per year, making them the second largest natural source of methane emissions. Methane is produced in termites as part of their normal digestive process, and the amount generated varies among different species."

9. If You Hold Them In, They'll Just Come Out When You Sleep

Even if you clenched your butt and held them in all day, the gas will escape once you relax. What's more relaxing than sleep?

10. People Even Fart After Death

Here's proof that you can't escape passing wind, even after you're dead! Up to three hours after the body dies, gasses continue to escape from both ends of the digestive tract, resulting in burping or farting noises. This phenomenon is due to muscles contracting and expanding before rigor mortis sets in.

TRUTH#24 – The Cliché: What's Good for the Goose is Good for the Gander? True & False!

Men if you cheat with someone else when you're in a committed relationship stop expecting your mate to stay at home and not see anyone else. Expecting women to put up with doing without intimacy is totally tired, sexist, unrealistic, and extremely unfair. Likewise, (vice-versa), the same goes for women in committed relationships. If you want to be open to dating others in your relationship, then for better or for worse, your mate has the right to equally sow their oats as well. If you want exclusivity in your relationship, there's a fair price you must pay. That price is honesty by upholding your end when it comes to exclusive commitment.

So, if you're not brave enough to be honest about slipping around then you're a JERK! Don't be surprised when the same slipping around happens to you, or worse you lose the one you love forever because of a bitter soul-shattering break-up. If you want an open relationship to date others be man or woman enough to present that desire to your mate, before you do it. That way all the <u>chips are on the table</u> and you both can decide if you want to allow for dating others or break-off the relationship and remain friends. Everyone deserves the respect of being given the opportunity to choose.

CHAPTER 8

LOVE DEPRIVATION

What's Deprivation? **deprivation (de-pri-va-tion)** adjective

- **the disadvantage that results from losing something**

Synonym: <u>loss</u>

The quality of having an inferior or less favorable position.

Source: vocabulary.com

LOVE DEPRIVATION – Life Scenario #1

Dan is a kind and loving husband happily married for 11 years to Rosa, a bubbly and beautiful young woman. Together they have three budding kids between them, two mischievous boys and one cheery- eyed girl. They all live happily in a middle-class American neighborhood and participate in social activities with the neighbors in their community. The boys are a chip off the old block and mimic Dan's love of sports and church activities. The little girl Amanda loves hanging out with Mama Rosa shopping, creating lovely ceramics, and frequenting local art shows. What the community and children don't know is that Dan has not had intimate relations with his lovely wife Rosa in nearly two years.

Some months ago, Rosa was diagnosed with a rare brain disease that completely shuts off her physical arousal needs. It's a hormonal disorder which means Rosa is ok with never having intimate relations again. This causes intimacy to become a bothersome chore for Rosa, rather than a pleasurable experience. Dan tried repeatedly to reason with Rosa but she continues to repeal his romantic advances. Rosa's doctors say that unfortunately there's no known cure for her problem, but they can give her a few medical injections, and pills, to restore Rosa's deceased libido. The doctors determined that once Rosa started taking the medication she'd probably have to continue taking the pills for the rest of her life.

Rosa staunchly refuses to adhere to the doctor's advice and says, "I feel fine just the way I am, and the way our lives are right now. If you truly love me and the children Dan, you'll just have to accept it!" Dan feels like a rock in a hard place. Dan is a very passionate man and the prospect of having such a beautiful wife that he can never be intimate with again is very disturbing to him. He does not want to lose his lifestyle, leave his children, pay child support that may cripple him financially, and it would seem like to his community that he's a failure as a husband and father.

Question: What should Dan do?
    a. Give up intimacy forever
    b. Cheat on his wife
    c. Ask his wife if it's ok to see other women
    d. Leave his family life and start anew

e. Have an intimacy change
f. Commit suicide

LOVE DEPRIVATION – Life Scenario #2

It's a starry Saturday night and Jimmy and his son Derrick are on a long car ride home together after a basketball game. Jimmy is still celebrating the fact that his high school basketball star son Derrick hit the game winner at the buzzer, in the State Championship Final. Jubilation is blissful until a drunk driver slams into Jimmy's car in a violent head-on collision. The damage from the wreckage was so bad that it killed his son Derrick and the drunk driver that caused the accident. But, Jimmy was spared his life only to find out that his neck was broken and that he'd be paralyzed from the neck down – a paraplegic for the rest of his life.

Jenny, Jimmy's wife, was of course devastated at the loss of their only child, and the paralyzed state of her once athletic and vibrant husband Jimmy. The fatal accident nearly crushed Jenny's will to live. In their wedding vows, Jenny and Jimmy swore to stick by one another through thick and thin, but it was apparent that intimate relations would never be a part of their married life again. For 8 years, Jenny loyally attended to Jimmy's every need including bathing, feeding, and clothing her paraplegic husband without complaint. Other anxious men knew of her tough situation and they found Jenny's loyalty to her husband and her physical beauty enormously attractive.

Jenny's would-be suitors even cared about Jimmy's well-being, but Jenny was a young attractive woman wanting to be held and loved in a manly way. Even though Jenny tried not to, she oftentimes felt that the strain of

Jimmy possibly finding out that another man would do something for her that he couldn't might kill him from disappointment and grief. Jenny still loves Jimmy with all her heart and soul, since the very first day they meet. But, she's torn inside between living a loveless life without children, or continuing to suffer the loss of physical passion for many years to come.

QUESTION: What should Jenny do?

    a. Slip out and have intimacy with another man

    b. Ask her husband if it'd be ok to have casual intimacy

    c. Place Jimmy in a nursing home

    d. Divorce Jimmy and start over with a new husband

    e. Euthanize him in his sleep with a pillow

    f. Never have intimacy again

LOVE DEPRIVATION – Life Scenario #3

Jamie is a smart A+ student at a top-notch Ivy League college. Jamie wanted to wait until marriage to have a first intimate experience, but after a night of hard drinking at one of the campus Fraternity parties, inhibitions got lowered. Jamie's virginity was lost. Everything seemed to be ok until flu-like symptoms begin to develop that never seemed to go away. After a visit to the campus nurse and a blood test, Jamie found out that the test for the disease AIDS read positive. Needlessly to say, Jamie was very frightened and depressed at the prospect of not having a loving relationship in the future because of the possibility of passing on this deadly disease to someone else.

Day after day Jamie quietly suffered in sadness because being intimate and having children was forever ruled out in the future. Jamie finishes college with honors never telling anyone about the AIDS, and swears off intimate relationships for life. Jamie landed a dream job that guaranteed wealth and the only thing that's missing is a significant other to share a successful life with. By the way reader, if you are a woman, Jamie is a man, if you are a man, Jamie is a woman.

QUESTION: What should Jamie do?

a. Never have intimacy as not to pass on the AIDS virus

b. Have safely protected intimacy and never tell to avoid persecution

c. Tell and hope the partner will understand and stay

d. Have intimacy whenever he/she wants and let others be responsible

e. Find another AIDS victim and settle down

f. Die alone and lonely

These 3 Love Deprivation scenarios are based on true life **facts.** This sad list of love deprivation in relationships really happened. How long do you think you could presumably go without intimacy in your relationships due to physical ailment, mind games, or mental health issues? One month, two or three months, six months, a year, two years, three years? Some people go up to ten years or more before calling it quits, and the last time I checked no one can turn back the hands of time to re-live the past hard times. In life, there are no dressed rehearsals.

Love deprivation happens to people from all walks of life, but until you've literally walked in their troubled shoes you don't know what's going on their lives. Yet we pass judgments, never realizing that the shoe could be on the other foot. Sometimes in your life you may be placed in an impossible position with an impossible choice to make. Who will have compassion in your life if the unthinkable happens to you?

THE SAVIOR COMPLEX

Are you looking for a mighty moral Holy Man to love like the men that used to live ages ago? Men whose saintly deeds live on as rules to live by in your religious book of choice? Are you looking for that motherly paragon of virtue that raised, cooked, and cleaned for you? When your Mama was Queen in your household, did the world revolve around you?

This is the Savior Complex: The Savior Complex is a state of mind which means no one can ever come close or live up to the high standards of the life lessons you have been spoon fed by parents and/or religious people during your life.

This belief of moral perfection has become so engrained in your mind that each person you want to have a relationship with must live up to a certain pre-conceived perfection mold. The long deceased Holy Men may be the closest thing to God that you know, but they cannot reappear to marry you, they're dead. Even if the Holy Man did come back from the great beyond and asked you for your hand in marriage, would it be fair to your family and friends to suffer from the rest of the common riff-raff available for them to have relations with? In other words, it's impossible for men to live up to impossible standards.

You don't marry your holy book; you marry a human being. Only a human can give you the genetics needed to produce children and provide the time, financial resources, and intimacy you desire. God or the Universe has given you the best it can currently right now, and now's all you have. The past is for the past. What will your relationships be…truth or implausible fantasy? Men, if your mother is the apple of your eye, no woman will ever match and compare to that. The only way to have a woman like that is to transplant the mind of your mother into the body of another woman by a mad-scientist from a bad, B-rated horror movie. It's not going to happen! The object is to find a woman who loves and accepts you - for - you – because no woman can ever be as perfect as Mama.

In other words, no one says and does everything right all the time. Nope. No sir-re buddy. Through all the slings and arrows you'll face in life, stop making it harder on yourself with unrealistic expectations. Let sensible compassion and common sense guide your relationship decisions.

How and Why You Must Forgiving Past Transgressions

"The weak can never forgive. Forgiveness is an attribute of the strong."
Quote ~ Mahatma Gandhi

"He who forgiveth, and is reconciled unto his enemy, shall receive his reward from God, for he loveth not the unjust doers."

Parable ~ The Koran

"Be it known unto you therefore, Men and brethren, that through this man is preached unto you the forgiveness of sins."

Parable ~ The Holy Bible ~ Act 13:38

"If your life is not all you want it to be, it may be that you have some forgiving to do!"

Quote ~ Unknown

Even the great Guru's and Sacred Books speak of the importance of forgiveness. I'm not saying that you are not to be moved by the terrors of the world but if you won't forgive past transgressions negative energy will eventually engulf and eat away at you (inside and out). Not forgiving causes unnecessary personal mental, social, physical, and spiritual destruction. Pent-up anger, frustration, and hatred engulfs your life and becomes an excuse for living lifelong failures and causes people to justify their unfair treatment of others, usually, years after the original offender that terrorized them is long gone out of the picture called your life.

Thinking about past abuses and hating your abusers will not physically harm the perpetrator of the offenses that you wish had never happened to you. It just keeps you attached mentally to the negativity of the past. That's not good for you at all. Forgiveness is not for the benefit of the bad offender, it's for the benefit of you. To get free of the baggage of the past so that you can live powerfully in your present day and in your future days. During the creation of your acts of forgiveness you leave the realm of childish pain and suffering and enter a purposefully empowered adulthood. There is nothing childish in forgiveness. It's the remover of mental anguish and a pathway to spiritual salvation. That's Powerful!

If you will not intentionally look at how "not forgiving" keeps you trapped in the past, your emotional suffering will for certain be lifelong. You will suffer and cause innocent love ones around you to suffer because that kind of egotistical pain always demands a human sacrifice. So, who'll become your sacrificial victim? Your best friend, your family members, your co-workers, your children, or yourself? Pick out your victims now while you're reading this book. It may sound silly but that's what you'll do subconsciously (automatically), almost daily. You become the victimizer and the abuser yourself. Just like the sick pervert that abused you.

What is the REWARD in that? What kind of life is that? It's a life marred in pain, shame, and destroyed lives.

If you're in an abusive cycle, you have the power right now to free yourself from the negative energies streaming through your mind. Please trust in the wisdom of God, the Universe, or a power you consider greater than yourself (like the energy that keeps you breathing), to aid you in prayer or meditation to give you the strength to overcome your personal demons. I'm praying for you right now. You will beat back the demons inside and become a better person because of it. Receive it!

It is a scientific fact that negative energy and positive energy can't inhabit the same space at the same time. I personally can testify to the cleansing power of forgiveness (I had to forgive a lot of bad people). If not for the fact I learned the power of forgiveness, you wouldn't be reading this book right now.

"When angry, count to ten before you speak, if very angry, a hundred."

Quote ~ Thomas Jefferson

Let's all practice FORGIVENESS by controlling our negative emotions. Practice, practice, practice!

Negative Emotional Control Exercise (NECE):

Step #1 Write down all the things that immediately come to mind that make you angry, frustrated, sad, or anxious.

Example: My list.

* Ignorant people who refuse to for whatever reason get some self-help education about life and grovel around miserably all the time. (This excludes you of course because you acquired this book.) ☺

* People who cut me off in traffic. (I know it seems petty but I'm still human.)

* People who are late all the time and always have some lame excuse for doing it. (Uh ooh, I think I just made my own list.) Etc., etc… you get the point - whatever comes to mind.

Step #2 Now that you have your list asks these questions about each of them.

a. What is the REWARD? (From now on for the rest of your life be brave enough to take the time to honestly ask and answer this question. If the reward stinks you have made a poor choice and fix it as soon as possible.)

b. What does it do to promote peace in this world?

c. Why do I, or don't I feel guilty about this negative behavior?

d. Where do these negative emotions come from? (I.e. negative childhood experiences, drug abuse, sexually repressed desires, religious beliefs, family practices, or cultural bias.). If this is part of my program how can I control it without repressing it? (Look for healthy outlets and/or support groups to work things out.)

Step #3 Discuss your findings with yourself first and if you feel comfortable, discuss these findings with a non-judgmental confidant.

How do you know if your confidant is non-judgmental? Ask them! If they'll be judgmental find someone else. One way to be assured that they're trustworthy is to invite the confident to write out a list and participate in the negative emotion exercise with you. If their negative emotional list is not juicy enough they are probably not being forthright. Thank them for their time and move on, and find another confidant. Don't be deterred. Your well-being and peace of mind are at stake. The universe will find a way to aid you in your search for peace and happiness, I promise you.

The more you share yourself with genuine friends who will listen to your issues without judgment, you grow to understand yourself. The greater the control you gain over your emotions, the greater it increases your chances to be happy and a positive contributor to humanity. I will be so proud of you as well as those who love you.

Step #4 FORGIVENESS – THE MOST IMPORTANT KEY: Forgiveness is the most important part of controlling your emotions. Why? Simply, forgiveness releases us from internal suffering and in-turn - lessens the ability of one to hate - instead of love.

The act of forgiveness is the only thing that can free you completely of negative emotions and stops the vengeful cycle of harmful, negative, physical and verbal reactions towards others and yourself. "Not forgiving" is to unwittingly push away the people you love and care about the most. Locking away your divine celestial beauty in a blockade of emotional anguish imprisons your spirit and halts your "**Spiritual-Evolution,**" preventing you from becoming your better version of yourself. "How can I forgive when I could never do it before?"

Forgiveness is not as hard as we make it out to be. It's unnecessarily harder than it must be when we let the hurtful childish EGOTISTICAL emotions dictate our mental actions. Just realize that forgiving will vanquish a lifetime of suffering within you. If you can communicate with the people you wish to forgive don't be fearful, don't cop out, don't worry, and don't have expectations of what the other person's reaction will be. (Forgiveness via telephone is recommended.)

Force yourself to go through with communicating with the abuser anyway. Be strong! If you can't reach the people you need to speak to, to forgive, ask God (or a Higher Power) to help you forgive them. The Higher Power will assist you if you're sincere in the asking. Be brave and make a list of all the people who have ever wronged you in your life. Starting from childhood to present day. If you're like me in the forgiveness department you may need two blank sheets of paper. Remember forgiveness is for you - to free yourself. Do it now, or as soon as possible.

How to Prepare a FORGIVENESS LIST – People to Forgive (Past/Present/Deceased) possibly consisting of:

* Immediate Family (Parents) – The source of your life and beginning stages of your programming. THE MOST IMPORTANT TO FORGIVE.

If you can't start with forgiveness with your Immediate family I promise you if you need to forgive them and you do not, your suffering will never end and you can discontinue the forgiveness exercise right here.

* Immediate Family List – Mothers/Fathers, Brothers/ Sisters, Grandmothers/Grandfathers, Husband/Wife, Children

* Non-Immediate Family - Uncles/Aunts, Cousins, Friends

* Best Friends, Acquaintances, Coworkers, Peers

* Intimate Partner (past and present), i.e. Boyfriends/ Girlfriends, Husband/Wife

* Enemies – Usually the hardest people to forgive. Enemies are sick people who have violated you in the worst way. If you never talk to someone you trust implicitly or consult a professional psychological counselor about past abuses perpetrated by enemies so that you can forgive them, you will never be truly happy. In other words, you will abuse others and innocents will suffer at your hands.

Why? Because suppressing trauma filled emotions causes them to fester like an open wound that will not heal. If you need help to forgive, it's ok to seek professional help.

*Self-Forgiveness – Oftentimes we can forgive others and neglect to forgive ourselves. Usually when we have been a victim of abuse (and we all have), we do things to lash out and we become the perpetrator of negative actions toward others.

This is a terrible thing because how can you be happy engulfed in self-loathing? To err is human! Mistakes are made by us so that we can learn from them. So, stop being so hard on yourself and filled with regrets. Negative emotions like shame, depression, despair, and grief don't serve any of us for the better. Move on, move forward, and create a happier life for yourself. You can do it!

A Prayer for Self-Forgiveness - (You Must Forgive Yourself As Well):

Almighty creator of all things. I humbly ask you to please give me the strength, love, courage, and wisdom to know that I'm not perfect and that I will make mistakes, but I must not let my mistakes destroy my life and my love for humanity. Help me to help myself, so that I can help others to know courage, love, and peace. Thank you for giving me the gift of life. Please forgive me.

Clean the slate of life and start anew with positivism and self-empowerment. Remove the weight of the world from your spirit and truly live, brothers and sisters. To forgive opens the way for true Power, Sanity, Love, Life, and Happiness to flourish in your soul. For Pete's sake do the exercise because it really will help. This is a scientific and spiritual fact! Appreciation without application is a recipe for failure. Only action with knowledge, will give you the satisfactory results you wish to manifest in life.

"If you are unhappy, you are too high up in your mind".
Carl Jung

"Because 'I love you' doesn't give you the right to abuse me! Just because you are my mate, my friend, my sister, my brother, my boss, my co-worker, my client, my president; Just because I'm your son, that doesn't give you the right to abuse me! I will still love you, but at a distance**."** ☺
Philosopher 'X'

CHAPTER 9

UNDERSTANDING REJECTION

What's Rejection: The act of rejecting something or somebody, (in other words a feeling of being loathed, hated, or a spit-in-the-face type of feeling).

Source: Philosopher 'X'

REJECTION is a big deal to humans and it holds the distinct title of being our number one mental fear in the world; Even greater than being eaten alive by zombies or becoming a homeless person.

Rejection is for all intents and purposes, is the opposite of love. And all of us want to love! We must learn to deal peacefully with rejection when it's directed at us. How you deal with rejection will sometimes be the difference between peace or anguish, happiness or sorrow, hate or love, and even life and death. Reject learning how to deal with rejection, at your own peril. People get physically disfigured every day because of peoples' inability to deal with relationship rejection issues. I wish we were taught how to deal with rejection in grade school curriculum because being a teenager in school with other teenagers - is tough. Perhaps if we were taught in school how to appropriately deal with rejection issues there'd be fewer funerals for our youth, fewer prisoners in our prisons, and more happy and productive college graduates.

Using the Keep the Peace - Mental Exercise Control (MCE) Featured in CHAPTER#4 - The Brain Part 2 Is one way to deal with Rejection, Anger, and Fear Issues.

READ ON TO SEE HOW TO DEAL WITH REJECTION ISSUES:

CHAPTER 10

THE NECESSITY OF CLUB ETIQUETTE

Dating in today's fast-paced world is a tremendous challenge and many of us wish our dating pursuits wasn't filled with unkind words of heartless rejection. But, people are not perfect by any stretch of the word. It's tough on men and women on the dating scene, but it can be especially tough on the man sometimes because in western cultures it's the social norm for the man to make the first introductory move when it comes to dating. Oftentimes the dating rule that men must ask for a date opens men up to scathing female rejection (ouch), unless he's a famous movie star, visibly wealthy, a powerful politician, or a musical rock, pop, rap, or R&B star, which seemingly gives these men exclusive dating rights to the ladies.

Still, dating is tough on the women too, who must work out whether a guy is worth her time, whether this guy is the one she will eventually marry, whether he's a playboy, or whether he's a crazy psychotic head-case intent on causing her harm. Yes, the dating scene is certainly tough on most people! Perhaps we need to broaden our understanding of the dating scene? Have you ever attended a class at school that taught you how the dating scene should go? Odds are you did not, but many of you have had classes on proper social etiquette (at least I hope so); *i.e.* ...what fork to eat the salad with and to keep your arms off the table.

Why not combine a social event, like going out to the club, bar, church, or another social arena with a more structured way of meeting and talking to people? Taking out the stressors of striking up that crucial initial conversation. I submit to you, for your approval, the following lesson in etiquette:

CLUB ETIQUETTE

Club Etiquette is a simple dating system developed by the Relationshipologist – Philosopher 'X', to ease the strain of meeting potential suitors in any social public setting. Using these simple tools, as well as engaging in friendly and informative verbal communication, you'll enhance cooperative civility with others at public gatherings. So, let's begin...

As a Relationship Expert, one of the biggest complaints I get from people is that it's too hard to meet new people and start a conversation. Let's face it... no one likes rejection. If you're out in public and you're clueless as to whether that attractive person you're eyeing is with their family members, or their significant other... How would you know? Exactly, You Don't!

CLUB ETIQUETTE TOOLS – RESPECT RINGS or RIBBONS

1. Stainless steel or plastic **neon pink** ring
2. Stainless steel or plastic **neon red** ring
3. Stainless steel or plastic **neon blue** ring
4. Stainless steel or plastic **neon green** ring
5. If you don't have a ring ribbons of a similar color will work

What respect rings, or ribbons signify is your personal relationship status and if you're open to dating or already in a relationship. These brightly colored rings, which are easy to see and distinguish between, are worn on what is traditionally the wedding ring finger (the left hand – 3rd digit from the thumb). This will let any interested suitors know whether to approach you, or leave you alone. Delightfully simple and effective!

Neon PINK ring (for single ladies) – means I am single, open to introductions and having a fun time, but you must respect my decision if I do not want to be with you.

Neon RED ring (for single men) - means I am single, open to introductions and having a fun time, but you must respect my decision if I do not want to be with you.

Neon BLUE ring (for married ladies) – means I am happily married, but I'd still like to dance or socialize with no intention of anything other than that.

Neon GREEN ring (for married men) - means I am happily married, but I'd still like to dance or socialize with no intention of anything other than that.

BEWARE! If the person does not have a **RESPECT RING** on and it's the practice in the establishment to wear a ring, if you choose to approach that person proceed with caution because they may be unavailable, or just looking to take out their frustrations on an unsuspecting suitor. This simple system incorporating **RESPECT RINGS** once made known to the public, makes dating and having fun easier. If you frequent a certain club, bar, or any other social establishment in which people like to meet, then you may want to strongly suggest that they make this system available to the patrons and have the rules of engagement advertised for all to see on their website, door entrance, etc. And they can even supply the rings, or their ribbon equivalents.

HAPPY DATING!

CLUB ETIQUETTE CONVERSATION

Now that we've established the ground rules and have the Club Etiquette Ring displayed and easy to see, let's establish a more structured form of first-time conversations at Club Etiquette Events… First and foremost, for Club Etiquette to work this one rule must apply:

Number One Rule of Club Etiquette - Always present yourself in a positive, friendly, and respectful manner, and be prepared to take 'NO' for an answer, without any hostility.

Rule#2 You must talk to each other in a friendly and honest way from the very beginning, and if you're the person initiating the first contact - if the person you've contacted says you're not their type or they're not interested in you, you must respect their wish and remain a perfect gentlemen or dignified lady in your conversations. By the way ladies, men love it when you make the first move. So, if you like what you see, you might want to be the first to initiate the conversation.

Examples of How to Talk to One Another:

Hello my name is _____, do you mind if I talk to you for a minute? (Proceed with the conversation as a nice and respectful Lady or Gentlemen)

If they say I'm here to meet people, but sorry you're not my type.

You are to respect their decision say 'thank you' and move on. Do so without questioning him or her for the reason why, trying to force a different outcome. If he or she says "you are not my type but we can be friends", then just be friends. Also, if a person agrees to dance or just chat with you, don't have unrealistic expectations that you're meant for each other and therefore must remain exclusive. People are free to socialize with others without you interrupting them. Honesty is key! Please people, try very hard not to take a rejection personally. If a person does not want you for a relationship - it's ok - and not the end of the world. There are over 7 billion people on the planet so you have billions of opportunities to find someone who will love you for you. So, be diligent, nice, and respectfully to each other from now on, ok?

Rule#3 Again if you get along with each other don't become overbearing, if the man or woman wants to dance or meet with others, it's ok.

Don't be pushy with someone you're attempting to date because that is a sign that you are possessive, desperate, or worse - crazy. No matter what, maintain your dignity and be respectful. It's ok to ask someone for their phone number if you're vibing on each other's company, but if they don't want to give out the digits, or they say "I'd rather you give me your phone number instead", then be fine with doing that if you want to. This proves to the person you're interested in that you're willing to compromise in the hopes of getting to know each other better. Remember, if they want to meet other people at the event that's ok. You can meet other people also without it being something bad or wrong. **Never - ever be rude or insulting under any circumstance!**

This concludes the three simple rules of Club Etiquette:

Respect Ribbons/Rings make for creating a much friendlier dating environment. So, help spread the word that it's cool to be respectable men and women on the dating scene. We all can use this type of community cooperation today while we have civilized fun doing it!

NOTE#1: Whether you're looking for a romantic relationship or you're already in one; it's ok to socialize with others in public encounters as long as interactions are conducted in a respectful manner. It's ok to be sociable and trusting of each other. It's time for love to thrive!

NOTE#2: Just because you meet someone with a date-ribbon on, do your due diligence and check out the person to make sure they're being truthful and authentic.

Internet Background Checks, Word of Mouth from other people, whatever… Just investigate or you might end up taking a long walk off a short pier. In other words, always be cautious of possible deceivers and psychopaths trying to take advantage of you. Don't get the wool pulled over your eyes - be smart and investigate your dates.

How to Appropriately Deal With Rude People

It's inevitable that in the dating world you'll occasionally run into rude people whenever you interact with others in a public setting, this is always a prevalent fact of life. So, how should you deal with rude people, without it ruining your day, and causing a massively overblown situation?

First Let's Understand Why People Are Rude to Begin With:

Why are people rude? People are rude because they're suffering from past abuses that have nothing to do with you. Somewhere in life they suffered painful abuse that came in the form of a bad relationship consisting of mental, physical, or emotional abuse from someone they felt powerless to do anything about. Only hurt people, wish to hurt other people. That's a scientific fact. Unfortunately, if you're being verbally assaulted by a rude person, it's not you. It's someone lodged in their subconscious mind that they're attacking. Rude people have not forgiven past indiscretions that victimized them in their earlier lives. In other words, be the better person and walk away during a seemingly senseless rude confrontation with a rude person, and don't take it personally. I know this sounds hard to do but you'll be a better and happier person for it. Please walk away.

Let's practice how to appropriately deal with rude people:

You're in a dance club and you see a beautiful woman or man bobbing their head to the beat. You find them interesting and you want to start a friendly conversation. You begin to talk to him or her, "Excuse me, I'm (your name), how are you doing?"

The rude person responds, "Get away from me! Get out of my face! (Expletive, expletive!)

This kind of reaction hurts your feelings and makes you want to punch the person.

Your reaction is this: (Smile and don't say another word). Quickly back away and when you're at a safe distance, walk away. That's it!

That's it! Pat yourself on the back because you've proven to yourself that you're a smart, decent, and forgiving human being. Now you can move on to meet someone better. That's after you calm down a bit from the rude person and enjoy further dating. Practice this with a friend or family member before you go out. Have them be rude to you and call you every bad name in the book as they pretend to be the person who you're interested in. It'll be great fun and you'll be prepared to deal with rude people and live to love another day.

The Exception to the Rule - When It's Ok to Be Rude:

It's ok to be rude if you've been polite to someone who approaches you and they continue bothering you by refusing your polite *no thanks* to their advances. If your feeling threatened, proceed to an available security guard and point out the rude offender. Some people are mentally unstable, so it's better to be safe than sorry. Later, if you're leaving the establishment it's ok to ask security to escort you to your awaited mode of transportation. Please be sure to look around your surroundings to make sure you're not being followed. Keep your wits about you and be safe.

CHAPTER 11

THE SECRET OF MEN

Ladies have you ever asked the question, "I just don't understand men?" It's time to clear the air on this matter once and for all… the secret of Men:

Men are just little boys in adult bodies.

That's right Ladies; men are still boys, now and forever! Men still love nice new shiny cars, playing games with the boys, having cookouts, being recognized for accomplishments big and small, and they also expect you to be their mother figure from time to time. Knowing all this, how do you make a man happy?

Simple: Treat him the same way as you'd treat your little boy, nephew, or cousin when they're the tender age of seven. This does not mean to blow their nose or wipe their butt. It means to dote over them when they do nice things for you. Even if you don't like the gift. It's ok to pretend you like it if the gift was given with good intentions from the heart. Hang out with your man sometimes when he's out with the boys. But give him some run around space with his friends every now and then. It's ok to put your foot down if the man goes overboard with hanging out. Men will not admit to it, but they respect a little authority from their mates when they get out of line.

One other thing Ladies: When you go out with your man to a gathering of his friends, dress classy, but not too revealing. Men love to show you to their family and friends so that they will wish they were in his shoes. Men love it when other guys tell him, "Bro you're a lucky man to have a woman like that". If your man doesn't like you to look nice and is overly jealous - **beware** something is terribly wrong with him. Run Away!

The number one thing a lady needs to know about a man: He needs to feel appreciated above all! (Preferably a little bit every day).

If a man thinks that his lady does not appreciate him and the things he does for her - matters not; It's only a matter of time that your romantic relationship together will come to an end.

It's like a mathematical equation... not appreciated + unhappy with the things I do for her = BREAK-UP!

CHAPTER 12

THE SECRET OF WOMEN

Men, have you ever asked the question, "I just don't understand women?" It's time to clear the air on this matter once and for all - the secret to women:

Women are just little girls in adult bodies.

That's right Men, the ladies still love to play dress up, style their hair, go shopping, play with babies as if they were dolls, love gossiping, are crazy for shoes, love receiving gifts, and like hanging out with other girls from time to time.

How do you make a woman happy?

Simple: Treat her the same way you would treat your little girl, niece, or cousin when they're the tender age of seven. This of course does not mean being condescending or bossy.

It means being tender, protective, loving and thoughtful.

Men, by nicely noticing when they get their hair fixed to look good for you, by complimenting them when they put on nice clothing or a new outfit, telling them how delicious their cooking is, holding hands while walking in the park, having small talk every day (even if it doesn't seem that important to you), and letting them know how beautiful they are (inside and out), is a must to make ladies happy. When you have disagreements, listen intently. But if it's not right in your mind then be a man and stick to your guns about why you disagree. But please don't be mean about it.

Let her hang out with her friends, (even guy friends), without being a crazy jealous fool. Believe me, if a woman gets tired of being with you she'll most certainly, very visibly let you know. Everyone needs space to themselves from time to time, so create trusting relationships together. It's ok to be apart sometimes.   Also, she needs to know and believe that you respect her opinion and that you view her as your intellectual equal in the relationship. Making your lady feel empowered and important is critical in a relationship.

The number one thing a guy needs to know about a woman: You need to let her hear you *verbally* say, without fail, weekly (or daily), these three words: *I Love You.* I don't care how mucho-macho you are, the words of love need to be communicated weekly or daily. Verbalized physically, with your mouth parts, without fail!

If you don't do this and she starts thinking something's awry, be prepared to lose your lady Bro!

Ladies, men are sometimes not smart enough to do this on their own because of the way they were reared as young children. So, it's ok to issue a friendly *do you love me* reminder every now and then. The key words here Ladies are 'friendly reminder'. Please remember, men are just big boys? ☺

Now before all the adults get too upset at Philosopher 'X' for calling them children. Please let me explain my reasoning:

CHAPTER 13

CHILDHOOD ADULTS EXPLAINED

Scientifically and psychologically the basis for everyone's behavior is based on what they learned about life growing up. When you feel anger, love, or anything else, it's because you experienced the same emotions and responses when you were young and these feelings are recycled, over and over, as time goes on and you grow into adults. Your emotional reactions are based on many interpretations that you learned as a child. To separate your childhood from your current identity would effectively turn you into an emotional amnesiac with nothing left in your mind to determine how to respond to life situations.

In other words, if you had no childhood to base your future feelings on, it'd be like having a book with no beginning, just an end. So, you wouldn't know how to react" to the now moments" without the feedback of learned childhood responses. Got it? Hence you are a child in an adult's body. The intelligence that governs our mental systems does largely function through the emotional perspectives we learned as children. We are forever tied to our childhoods. Just because we have bigger adult bodies that can be intimate, make cute little babies, and tend to boss each other around, doesn't mean were 100% adults.

It'd greatly enhance your quality of life if you embraced this fact. Why?

Being the eternal child has a lot of benefits because you're happiest when you're the most playful and childish! But like anything else, everything has a - yin and yang - or - good and bad - side. Being childish in a brat-like, mean, stubborn way is awful! Look at the world's governments! They're big brats! I literally believe that ten-year-olds could be better politicians and get more political things done in our government for the benefit of everyone. Anyway... The goal in life is to be happy and peaceful 'childhood adults'. We only need to be serious when we should be to solve certain serious life problems. Have fun, be childish, and the universe happily smiles with you! ☺

CHAPTER 14

A NEW PARADIGM

For better or worse, a new paradigm has occurred in the world of relationships. If we want to co-exist peacefully we must become open-minded to engage in new insightful and inventive ways of communicating to solve relationship conflicts. If this doesn't happen, then I fear the worse for humanity. By golly if the worse happens, "I'm a Human too!" The true paradigm shift that has occurred is that women are more educated now than in any other time in recent history. Modern women are no longer willing to tolerate the unfair actions suffered by their female ancestors in the past.

There are two possible routes you can take in today's relationships:

1. Leave what society considers normal alone and see if you can take a different approach to relationships that will work for you.

2. Stick with the norm and hope that it'll become a successful relationship model for you.

The Following are Past and Present Day Marriage and Commitment Models:

- Arranged marriages by parents, guardians, or caretakers
- Male with multiple wives
- Wife with multiple males
- Male with wife, concubines, mistresses, or slaves
- Man and Wife - open polygamous marriage with shared or unshared partners
- Committed relationship without marriage
- Man and Wife without any intimacy relations due to religious beliefs
- Man kidnaps a woman and forces her into marriage
- Woman is sold by parents or guardian into marriage
- Traditional one man - one woman monogamous marriage

These relationship models have been practiced throughout human history, believe it or not, these relationship models are still in practice somewhere in the world today. Perhaps in your very own community. Some relationship models are successful on a person to person basis, and others are not. Depending on the outcome of what you perceive the outcome of a successful relationship to be. The thing about these relationship models is that if you haven't experimented with one of them it's brand new to you, no matter how long they've been around in human history. So, what will your model for success in a relationship be?

How to find Mr. or Ms. Right - and which model will be the model I choose to experiment with in my relationships?

In the world of relationships, schemers, con-artists, liars, gold-diggers, and crazy people abound. Everyone seems to be out for themselves and fair play and honesty can be lost in the mix. People figure out what to say to you (what you like to hear), to get what they want from you. Even if they want you for something as sacred and serious as marriage. This is the reason that divorces and break-ups are at epidemic proportions, because the reasons for the relationships are founded and based on selfish, untruthful desires. Oftentimes, people believe that they're telling you the truth because they want it to be true, so very badly. So, they figure telling little white lies will probably not hurt and won't matter. People tend to think that if they love and care for you enough that everything will work itself out and be ok. Wrong. Building a relationship on a stack of cards (or lies), will eventually crumble. It's only a matter of time. Be it one year, three years, five, ten, 20, or 30 years. When the relationship falls, it falls hard! Scarring your loved ones' emotions for a very long time. In most cases because relationships become so emotionally and financially entwined it leads to destroying families and careers. Betrayal of the heart is very hard for human beings to forgive.

BEWARE: Common Lies People Use to Get What They Want Out of a Relationship

1. **I love you.** Beware if they speak of love too soon. It must feel right to you.

2. **I had the money, but an emergency came up!** If this happens too many times the person is using you for your money. It's all about the money.

3. **I love kids!** If a person doesn't want to participate

in quality time with your kids be wary. Also, if they want to spend too much time with the kids (especially men), that may be a danger sign as well. Don't be blinded by love. Keep your wits about you.

4. **I will quit a certain annoying behavior when we're married!** A relapse of bad behavior is inevitable. People must get out of the habit of thinking that they can change people - it doesn't work! No matter how much you love them. Stop enabling and rewarding bad behavior by sticking around in a relationship when you should be long gone. Don't get stuck on stupid!

These lies are fine to live with if you're a glutton for punishment. If all you really want is some temporary companionship and don't mind them not being in love with you then it's your right to live that way, if you choose. People are what they are. It's up to you to decide if lies and bad behavior is something you're willing to put up with within your relationships.

CHAPTER 15

ATTRACTION

Everyone wants to know what's attractive to the opposite sex. Here it goes:

What Women Are Attracted To:

- The Number #1 thing women are attracted to about men is – Confidence! Guys even if you must pretend that you're confident, you've got to be confident in yourself. Women love confidence even more than physical looks. (Women like looks too, but exuding high amounts of confidence will get you a pass). Ever seen a beautiful woman with an ugly guy? Confidence!

The 4 Sure Signs of Confidence Women Look for in a Man

- Despite what most guys think, the signs of confidence that great women look for in a man have nothing to do with acting "tough" or "dominant."

- I've said it a bazillion times…great women don't see a man as potential "relationship material" based on his looks, money, or cheesy pick-up lines.

- When it comes to figuring out if a particular guy might be "Mr. Right," the first thing most women look for are sure signs of confidence. More specifically, the four unmistakable, magnetic signals that confident men send a woman the moment they meet her.

- Naturally, a man doesn't need to show them all to get the attention of a great woman…but if he manages to show her just a few, chances drastically increase that she'll start "feeling it" for him.

- 1) **An "Easy-Going" Attitude**

- Listen…"easy-going" does not mean being so laid back when you first meet a woman that you're practically asleep. It also doesn't mean putting up with any kind of rude or inappropriate behavior. It means handling the opinions, pressures, and attitudes of others with grace, and coming across as comfortable in your own skin. Even your body language communicates it…a confident man will literally, physically "lay back," leaning back while keeping his body open and facing forward when conversing.

- A confident man also doesn't obsess about what other people think or do. He doesn't take it as an insult if someone doesn't like him, or disagrees with him. Above all, he isn't needy, <u>clingy</u>, and always trying to be the center of attention. Basically, this "easy-going" attitude signals a woman that a man is the leader of his own life.

- 2) **He's "Put Together"**

- It's true, a woman will never decide that a man might be "Mr. Right" just because he looks like Brad Pitt…but rest assured she'll instantly rule him out if he doesn't look "right"…caring about himself enough to attend to the basics of appearance which communicate a positive, healthy self-image.

- Again, this doesn't mean that a man has to buy trendy clothes…wear a "scent"…or look like an obsessive gym rat. It does mean that he needs to master the basics of good grooming and hygiene. Because, if a man doesn't have it together enough to attend to his own needs, a quality woman knows right away that there's no way he can possibly attend to hers.

- Finally: coming across as "put together" means <u>communicating confidence</u> about who you are on the inside as well. You can do it by being able to carry on an interesting conversation about music…food… culture…whatever. Becoming a good conversationalist is a sure sign that you have it all together…that you're in a healthy, curious, confident state of mind.

- 3) **He's Humble**

- This is a big one. Like I always say, any "jerk" can act cocky with a woman…but coming across as confident requires something else: the ability to control what you say and do so that you never come across as "above" anyone else.

- For example, it's okay to look across the room at some other guy and say something cocky like, "Look at that guy's facial hair…I think 1975 wants it back." But ONLY if he's HUMBLE enough to add a comment like, "Believe me, I know…mine was just like it."

- **4) He Has A Sense of Humor**

- File this one under "No-Brainer"…a great sense of humor is the most instant, obvious, magnetic force that makes a Woman sense a man's confidence… and therefore feel the first sparks of attraction for him.

- That's why I suggest that guys do whatever they can to cultivate a "comic sensibility", even it means just reading a few books about the theory and structure of comedy and timing.

- I also recommend checking out cutting-edge humor sites like "Funny or Die" and "The Onion," or just watching "Saturday Night Live" to understand what's hip and funny…because it's all guaranteed to change and become "lame" tomorrow.

- Add it all up, and the message is clear:

- While most men waste time trying to impress women by acting "tough" or "dominant"… the signs of confidence great women look for are much more subtle… and much more easily achieved.

- By focusing on "broadcasting" the four signs of magnetic "real-man" confidence…the kind of women you want to meet will start sensing that you just might be "Mr. Right."

SOURCE: David DeAngelo ~ Author ~ Dating Secrets

- Women are attracted to protectors. Men I recommend if you're not a Bruce Leroy, Jackie Chan, Jet Li, or Steven Segal type Martial Artist, that you invest in non-lethal self-defense weapons (i.e. electric hand-held stun guns and pepper spray), that you keep on your person when you're out in public or secluded places. Let your lady know that you have protection and I also suggest that you get her the same self-defense weapons that you have so that she can protect herself and, watch your back. Be sure that you both know how to take weapons off '*safety*' and learn how to use them properly to be safe. So, until you learn how to be proficient in Jujitsu and Thai Kick-Boxing, get the self-defense gear and make sure you're always aware of your surroundings.

What Men Are Attracted To:

- You guessed it - Looks! But ladies there's a catch. You don't have to be the prettiest or the fittest for men to be attracted to you. Just dress to impress, have a great smile, be willing to listen to guys' conversations, and be authentic about how you feel about people, places, and things. In other words, have a positive attitude and look as good as you can with what you were born with. I promise men will love you! Men will drop a beautiful woman like a hot potato if she has a rotten condescending attitude.

- Also, men are attracted to good hygiene, a woman with great social skills (i.e. helpful in meeting people, and socializing especially in business), and willing to lend an occasional helping hand to her mate after a long day of stress, and willing to occasionally lend a helping hand with charitable contributions to the community.

THE SIMPLE SHORT MR. or MS. RIGHT LIST - (What to Look For In A Mate)

This is a unisex list - that means it applies to both Men and Women

- A good sense of humor
- Is honest even if you don't agree
- True to their convictions but willing to listen and can accept being proven wrong
- Good hygiene is a must
- A person who allows you to be yourself and makes suggestions - not commands - about how you should behave
- Shares in the cooking, cleaning, and household chores if needed without fuss
- Listens to what you want in the intimacy department without being pushy
- Secure enough to trust you with alone time with yourself, family, and friends
- Loves children even if they're not biologically their own
- Willing to show love and commitment through sincere words and pleasant actions
- Helps with finances (within reason), before you're even serious about a long-term commitment

- A person who's a loyal companion and friend and got your back when the chips are down

This is a simple list to follow and all the other stuff people expect out of relationships may serve to confuse and muddle their relationships. Confusion in a relationship creates problems in relationships. Best to know all you can about each other early in the relationship bonding process. Now, mind you, it is extremely rare to find these qualities in men under the age of 40, and women under the age of 30, due to active imaginations, libidos, and hormones still at their peak. So, the key to having long-term relationships, if you're between 18 and 30 years old is to be as honest as possible. I also suggest that once you've committed to a long-term serious relationship that you attempt to live with each other for at least 3 years and don't have children during this important transformative endeavor. Do this "3-year test" before settling down to possibly cut-out the possibility of living a lifetime of despair. 3 years is not that long in a lifetime to be sure that your life-mate is the right choice.

This gives young couples valuable time to learn about life in general and to clearly see if you're going to have second thoughts or change your minds about the commitment. If you'll be able to live with each other within the mix of the ensuing emotions that you'll encounter in life, then it must be a match made in heaven. It's tough to be honest in relationships sometimes but it's better to be in a joyful situation rather than becoming bitter enemies because you feel that you have been deceived in love.

NOTE: Brother's and Sister's its ok to make mistakes – even in relationships - mistakes are how we learn about each other and about life. But never settle for Mr. or Ms. Wrong - You deserve better than that.

FACING THE FACTS
All relationships will not work out and odds are most will not work out!

Some relationships will only work for a little while, or several years. No matter how deep your love is, or how honorable your commitment to a unified outcome may be. It does hurt when an avalanche of negative emotions flood into your mind when your suffering through the tough monuments leading to a relationship break-up. It seems like you're going to lose your mind! Oftentimes, we have desires of vengeance against our mate for the break-up turmoil that they've put us through. Believe me, I know.

It hurts badly and there's no quick fix for a broken heart, but we must live in the world together. Even though ending close relationships with people you love and care about is a maddening prospect, I promise you the break-up doesn't have to leave a lingering legacy of torture on your mind, body, and spirit. Learn to be forgiving and take some personal time to regroup. Eventually, odds are that you'll find love again. Just be smart and choose as best you can and when you do choose don't move too fast. There's no rush. The truth of the matter is there's no easy formula to ensure that you'll not have snags or failures in your relationships. Many men and women won't ever be fully committed and faithful in relationships. It's just not in them.

If a mate wants to be with other people it'll happen no matter what restrictions you put in place. People think they can sternly insist that their partners stop infidelity from occurring, but that's usually a bigger fairytale than Jack and the Beanstalk. Maybe teaching our children about prince charming and valiant knights just proves to confuse them about the reality they'll experience in future relationships?   For the men and women who choose not to be faithful I ask you to consider the different marriage models mentioned before. Conventional and unconventional. Honestly and fairly negotiate terms with your partner or partners from a different type of relationship point of view. It may take a lot of time and an abundance of personal resources to make a partner or multi-partner commitment a reality, but past human history has proven it can be done. All relationships are problematic so it might as well be the type of relationship you want. Mind you, I'm not putting one form of commitment as being more righteous or dominate than the other. I leave it up to you to decide which commitments are your equal opportunity love choices.

INTERESTING FACT: In the country of Mexico, you can get married for 2 years and after 2 years you can renew the marriage for 2 more years or call it quits. This way you can dissolve the marriage with no big divorce squabbles or lengthy court battles.

CHAPTER 16

HOW TO LIVE TOGETHER WITHOUT KILLING EACH OTHER

Now That You've Found Your Mr. or Ms. Right and You Have Committed to Start Living Together; How Do You Do Live Together - Successfully?

Believe it or not, there are certain unimplied or implied female/male and expectations mentally in place in our minds of what we expect to happen when we domicile (live) together. Why? I don't specifically know. But I do know, if you do not follow the "How to Live Together Lists" I created… Take my word for it, you'll be in a lot of trouble attempting to live in a happy home without taking heed of these following lists. Here they are:

How to Live Harmoniously With a Woman List

Ok guys you're happy to have found the one and you've won her heart. Congratulations! Now that you live together here is a listing to hopefully ensure your success with relationship bliss:

1. **Most Important Rule Of All** – PUT THE TOILET SEAT BACK DOWN! It drives women berserk?

Why? I don't know but this is key. Just Do It!

2. Keep the Home Clean

- Always flush the toilet and don't urinate on the toilet seat. (If you do wipe it off ASAP).

- Don't put dirty socks or clothes on the floor. (Put them in a hamper ASAP).

- **IMPORTANT NOTE:** Never leave trimmed hair in the bathroom sink! Never leave hair in the bathtub or shower! This Drives Women NUTS!

- Occasionally and voluntarily wash the dishes and clothes.

- **(See End of This List For Info on How To Wash Clothes).**

3. Men Must Take Out the Garbage

- This is 100% the Man's Job! It's never Ok to let a woman take out the Garbage. Why? Who knows that's just the way it is. Just Do It!

4. Ask Her About Her Day – And Listen and Respond Attentively

- Quality Communication is key with Females. Why? Scientist theorizes that women created speech. Also, that women can seemingly speak thousands of more words than men can in a day. Therefore, ladies have to speak a lot of words to be satisfied with a conversation.

(So, even if you're not interested in how their day went - if you want peace in your home, be interested).

• Tell Her You Love Her Often, and Mean It.

5. It's Ok to Be a Little Jealous – But Not A Lot

• Guys stop being so possessive. You must have trust in your woman. Let her go out and have fun sometimes. It's fine as long as she comes back home to you.

6. Compliment Her On Her Looks

• Women love to look good for their men and they love it even more when you compliment them on the beautiful appearance of their hair, nails, perfume, shoes, etc… So, compliment the ladies.

• Compliment her on her cooking even if it's not great. (I just season the food when they're not in the kitchen). ☺

• Never, ever, ever, ever, - Call her FAT! That's a deal breaker for women. If she asks "Does my butt look fat in this outfit?" – Immediately say NO!

"WORDS are Sword spelled backward."

Quote ~ Ralph Smart – YouTube Guru – Infinite Waters

"Hell, hath no fury like a Woman scorned!"

Quote ~ William Congreve

7. Women Despise Broke Men (Men With No Money)

- Once I, 'X', had a conversation with an older lady about what she didn't like about men. To my surprise she told me that she got tired of men being broke (no money), all the time. She stated, "I really love and respect men but it's frustrating when we can't even go out and enjoy each other's company for worrying about how much stuff costs." I understood then that when a man can't contribute financially it saddens and frustrates our women. So, Brothers you don't have to be rich but you do need to be able to contribute financially in relationships when you can.

- Men if you're ambitious in making strides towards making more money to become financially stable, then a good woman will work with you. Otherwise get ready for BIG problems around money. **(I recommend all Men & Women look at Money Videos by Bob Procter on YouTube).**

IMPORTANT NOTE FOR MEN: It's time for men to stop chasing quantity in women and start looking for quality in women. Quality makes for better relationships. Womanizing isn't cool any more Guys.

How to Wash Your Clothes - SOURCE: WikiHow

Follow these steps and you'll be a washing (and drying) wiz in no time.

Using a Washing Machine and Dryer (Don't Mess Up the Clothes! Follow Instructions or Else!)

a. **Sort your clothes into piles.** When washing clothes, there are two main things to keep in mind: what the color of the clothes are, and what material they are made out of. Not all fabrics can handle the same amount of water pressure or level of tumbling.

- Separate light and dark colored clothes. When you wash your clothes, especially new clothes, some of the dye used on the fabric will run out of the clothes (that's why older clothes have a more faded color than bright, new clothes.) Any clothes that are white, cream, or a light, pale pastel color, should go in the 'whites' pile, while all other colored clothes should go in the 'dark' pile. If you don't separate, your new bright blue shirt might dye all of your white clothes blue.

- Separate your clothes based on the fabrics they are made out of. Some fabrics, like denim or thick cloth (like a towel) need to be washed on a heavier wash cycle than your silky lingerie (which gets washed on a delicate setting.) You should separate your clothes by the sort of wash cycle their fabrics are meant to be washed in.

- Remember, towels and sheets should not be washed together. The top load washing machines should be used for towels, and sheets should be washed in front load machines (They are less harsh on sheets so they come out with fewer wrinkles).

b. **Read the 'care tag' on your clothes.** The cloth tags are not just sewn into clothes to make your neck itchy when they rub against your skin-- they're actually there to help guide you through the washing process. When in doubt about how to wash an item, check the tag. The care tags tell you what fabric the item is made of, how it should be washed, and how it should be dried.

- Some clothes need to be dry cleaned or washed by hand (see Method Two for how to do this.) The care tag will tell you if either of these things is necessary.

c. **Know what water temperature to select.** Washing machines have different temperature settings because some fabrics and colors require different levels of heat to be washed thoroughly.

- Use hot water for light colors, particularly light colors that are especially dirty. The heat will scald the stains right out of those white items.

- Use cold water for dark colors, as cold water reduces the amount of dye that runs from these clothes (so your clothes won't fade as fast when you use cold water.) Cotton items should also be washed in cold water as they are less likely to shrink in cold water.

d. **Know what size load to select.** Most washing machines have a knob that you must turn to select the right size load for the amount of clothing you have (generally either small, medium or large.) If your clothes fill up one-third of the machine, you should select small. Two-thirds of the machine means you should select medium, and if you fill up the whole machine, you should select large.

- Never squish clothes down so that you can fit more in. You should just run another load with your extra clothes or else you could risk jamming the machine or damaging it in some other way.

e. **Know what washing cycle to select.** As with temperature, washing machines also have different types of cycles, as different kinds of clothing require a different level of washing.

- Regular/Normal cycle: Select this when washing white clothes. It will leave your white items crisp and fresh.

- Permanent press: Use this for your colored clothes. This cycle washes with warm water and ends with cooler water, which keeps your colors looking bright.

- Delicate: As you might guess, anything that is relatively delicate (bras, dry-fit wear, cotton sweaters, dress shirts, etc.) Always make sure that your delicates do not require you to dry-clean or hand wash them (check the tag to make sure.)

f. **Add the right kind of washing fluid and close the door.** Washing fluid includes detergent, bleach, and fabric softener. You can either add your clothes and pour the right washing fluid on them, or keep your clothes out of the washer, fill the washer ⅓ of the way with water, add the washing fluid, and then add the clothes.

- Detergent: The amount of detergent you put in your washing machine is determined by how large your load is. Generally, detergent lids act as cups that have marked off amounts. Generally, ⅓ of the cup should be filled with detergent for a small load, ⅔ for a medium load, and a full cup for a large load. However, read your specific detergent bottle for instructions on how to use that detergent-- some detergents are more concentrated than others, meaning you don't need to use as much.

- Bleach: Bleach is used when you want to get tough stains out of clothes, or you want your whites to be really, really white. There are two kinds of bleach. Chlorine bleach is good for really making your whites white but should never be used on any colored fabric. All-fabric bleach can be used on colored fabrics.

- Fabric softener: This is used when you like your towels extra fluffy. Fabric softener should be added during the rinse cycle. Some machines have a dispenser where you can pour the softener when you begin the wash cycle, and it will add it to the rinse cycle at the right time.

g. **Move your clothes to the dryer and select the right cycle.** Keep in mind that there are some clothes that should be air dried. Check the tag--if it says not to dry it, hang these items somewhere they can dry. Like the washing machine, the dryer also has settings that you have to wade through to dry your clothes. Add a dryer sheet and close the door.

How to Harmoniously Live With a Man List

1. Ladies Pretend You Like Sports

- Why do men like sports so much? Who Knows! But a man loves it when his lady half-way likes sports. (Especially Football and Basketball). Just watch and shout now and again and he'll love you for it! Believe it or not, some women love sports more than guys. Go Figure.

2. Let Him Hang Out With the Boys

- Guys like hanging out with the boys. So, trust him and let him go out with the boys without mean comments and vindictive bouts of eye-rolling. I'm not saying that hanging out with the boys should take precedent over your quality time. If a man hangs out with the boys more than 33% of his free time weekly, then you should politely ask him to cut it down a bit.

3. It's Ok to Be a Little Jealous – But Not Overly Jealous

- Ladies stop being so possessive. You must have trust in your man. Let him go out and have fun sometimes. It's fine as long as he comes back home to you.

4. Appreciate Him and His Heartfelt Gifts

- A lady friend of mine told me that she asked her husband to buy her a washer and dryer for the holidays but in his infinite wisdom he bought her a mink coat instead. Needless to say, this made her very angry because they had 2 small kids and she always did the laundry.

- I, 'X', told her men do mean good and have good intentions but sometimes we do stupid stuff and make stupid decisions. By her husband getting a totally impractical gift it caused her to lash out at him and they had a terrible argument over a mink coat. I told her that it would have worked better if she would've said thank you for the beautiful coat and afterward peacefully worked on getting him to see the benefits of the appliances she needed to wash clothes. That way there are no arguments, you both still love each other, and the clothes washing problem is peacefully solved. A win-win! ☺

5. Ladies Look Great – But Don't Be Too High Maintenance

- Men love it when their women look good and feel good without breaking the bank. It just rubs men the wrong way when it seems like you only covet material things and material looks. It makes men think you're shallow and uncaring about the real important issues in the world.

6. Ladies Prepare Food Every Now and Then

- A woman told me once she had no problem with being submissive in a relationship with a man. I wanted to tell her real men don't want a submissive woman; real men want a woman who doesn't mind occasionally serving her man in a way that is "Mutually Beneficial" to both. In other words, being a woman is assisting her man with kind occasional service but not being a submissive slave. That's way too boring in a relationship.

- In reality ladies, you don't even have to cook, just make sandwiches sometimes and pour a bowl of cereal, boil and peel a couple of eggs, and pick up some take-out food sometimes. If you like cooking sometimes, that's a major turn-on for men!

7. Be Forgiving: Men Find It Hard to Remember Important Dates, Anniversaries, & Holidays

- Ladies I promise you men don't forget dates

on purpose. For some unknown reason, men can't seem to remember important dates or even remember to make a note of important dates in their calendar planners. Why? I don't know.

So, my dear ladies please hint friendly reminders a month out, and then again a week out, before the important event. That way you'll get the attention, recognition, and appropriate gift you desire. Keywords ladies is "friendly reminders". Thanks!

IMPORTANT NOTE: Men/Women it's important that you become <u>flexible</u> in working to correct issues in relationships.

I.e. In a hurricane the strong rigid oak trees become uprooted and die, but the flexible palm trees give way to the storm winds but don't fall, and they live on and look beautiful doing it.

I.e. You place a big stone boulder in a flowing stream but the water just flows over and around the gigantic stone. Which one is stronger the stone or the water?

Therefore, in a relationship, the person who's rigid (stubborn unwilling to bend and compromise), is usually the trouble-making weakest link in a relationship. The person willing to listen, be flexible, and willing too fairly compromise in a troubling situation is typically the wisest and strongest in a relationship. Co-operative people tend to have better longer lasting relationships. Why? Because of their logical, fair, and flexible, approach to troubleshooting their relationship problems. It's not survival of the fittest that thrives – it's survival of the harmoniously cooperative that wins the successful prize of living a life full of beautiful loving relationships.

"You must be shapeless, formless, like water. When you pour water in a cup, it becomes the cup. When you pour water in a bottle, it becomes the bottle. When you pour water in a teapot, it becomes the teapot. Water can drip and it can crash. Become like water my friend."

Quote ~ Martial Arts Master & Movie Star - Bruce Lee

CHAPTER 17

THE AGITATION TEST

Men have you ever been in a relationship with a woman and out of left-field, for no apparent reason she does something so utterly illogical that it confuses you beyond belief? For instance, you both agreed on a place to eat out but now she says she doesn't want to go out anymore; or it's your fault that "I was late to the movie because you didn't let me get dressed in time"; or "why are you going out with the guys to the ball game again this week without inviting me first"; being falsely accused of committing numerous infidelities; or just anything that seems to agitate you over, and over, and over again?

You have just experienced the Agitation Test. The Agitation Test is a mental test that females instinctively do to test a man's temperament (how quick he is to anger). Why? Because women know that in most cases men are more physically powerful than them and if they're prone to becoming angry because of little things, then how will a man react when things become really bad? Men can physically harm women and if no one is around to step in during a violent altercation there may be little recourse available for the lady to stop a big strong man from harming her. Because if you're in a relationship together you both tend to be in the same room together - a lot and alone.

Violence by men on women is a very real possibility in a relationship. Unfortunately, domestic abuse happens to women every day. But we're going to change that.

Men you will be Agitation Tested! You will be agitated by the women in your life so deal with it with understanding, patience, and compassion. Men you will be tested by your wives, daughters, girlfriends, co-workers, and sometimes complete female strangers. Deal with it as calmly as possible, so you can to pass the agitation tests. Hopefully by calmly passing the tests you will halt more future test agitations from transpiring throughout your relationships. You will be tested so make sure you keep your calm and past the tests.

Women, I understand that you must investigate a man's temperament to see if he's ok to be with, but when you keep Agitation Testing a man he will think you're mentally unstable, and eventually find a way to end the troubling, vexing, and over-challenging relationship. Believe me, men talk to each other about how women agitate them, almost more than sports. So, ladies if you plan on having lasting relationships with men please stop letting the Agitation Test run on automatic. Understand that if your man passes several tests, stop testing him. Continuous agitation testing will create problems that are not even necessary, and you'll unwittingly ruin a perfectly great relationship.

Please! Stop being an Evil Queen by always dethroning your King because you can never fix a man with mind-games. Mind-Games like the Agitation Test does not work in the long-run in committed relationships. To ensure a long-lasting relationship only divine love, patience, and understanding allows a wise woman to gain the ability to give her man the opportunity to decide to change himself for the better.

NOTE: Everyone uses the Agitation Test in one way or another, but too much agitation being perpetrated on someone is emotional and mental abuse. Don't be an agitating abuser.

CHAPTER 18

LACK OF REFINEMENT AND INTEGRITY

Refinement - an addition or alteration that improves something or someone by making it more sophisticated or effective.

Integrity - the state of being sound or undamaged - the quality of steadfastly adhering to high moral principles and high professional standards.

Source: Philosopher 'X'

Refinement and Integrity - These two important characteristics are grossly missing in most societies of the world (and they probably always have been). That's why there are so many problems not only with relationships but with the world of mankind in general. Many of us were never taught to be honest enough with ourselves and others to enable us to truly function with refinement and integrity in our everyday lives. Sure, we're taught to be quiet inside the library and church, but when are you taught to be quite in a confrontation with a loved one to 'keep the peace' in your home? Wisdom in peace-making is to bring up the vexing matter at a later time of day, when both people are in a calm frame of mind.

Believe me, don't argue when you're eating or in the middle of something important, wait until a more opportune moment arises to work out the problem together and bring about a beneficial and respectful resolution to the problem. So, I usually wait to talk over problems in the late evening after dinner and right before bed. I usually start the dialog by asking, "Is it ok to talk now?"

What Happens When We Break-Up?

We live through most of our relationships in trial and error periods. Sometimes the trials are too hard, and the errors too great, to seem like being in a relationship is worth the effort. When the relationship becomes too much of a burden we break it off. Then there are divorce legalities, splitting -up financial resources and in worse case scenarios, loss of life and limb due to domestic violence circumstances. Unfortunately, kids who're stuck in the middle of adult break-ups feel that they're left with hardships of their own as well. Kids don't realize that the adult break-up is beyond their control and bitterness can settle into their impressionable minds making forgiveness and understanding near impossible in their future adult relationships.

Point Being: We can end the vicious cycle of awful relationships and hatred by making more responsible choices and mustering up the courage to be true to ourselves. Pre-factoring in the circumstances that'll make a difference in the onset of relationships such as finances, religious/ spiritual expressions, the state of health, and intimacy concerns, will be a big help in living within loving, long-lasting relationships. It'll be hard to do in a society set up to keep us separated through economics, religions, and racial stereotypes, but I assure you that the consequences of not thinking ahead and thinking wisely will lead to tremendous hardships, unhappiness, and years of lost time in your relationships. Think, use your brain, be smart, and create relationships that enhance and expand your life.

CHAPTER 19

THE GRAND DECONSTRUCTION

What's The Grand Deconstruction? The Grand Deconstruction is when your life falls apart and you're wondering why everything in your life is so volatile and crazy. Sounds Familiar?

The Ancient Story of the Wise African Farmer

Long ago in Africa, there lived a very prosperous African Farmer. The Farmer was a spiritual man and he wholeheartedly believed his great farming success came from his ability to pray, meditate, and visualize future vast crop harvest in his imagination, (repetitively visualizing that the crops already exited on his lands). Miraculously the Farmer's vivid daydreaming eventually manifested his visualizations into a successful farming reality.

The Farmer had a son and he wanted his son to know how to utilize use his father's mental visualizing practices to achieve farming success like he did. So, the Farmer created a mantra/prayer for his son that stated, "Everyday my life is filled with wealth, health, abundance, and happiness. Thanks, Great Spirit. I'm eternally grateful." Every day his son followed his father's advice and life on the farm was beautiful. One day to the Farmer's surprise, his son, now a young man, accidentally fell off his horse and broke his leg in three places. "How can this be!? "Cried the Farmer. The Farmer was perplexed about how his teachings of living a successful happy life went so horribly wrong and failed his beloved son.

Soon after the accident the Farmer's country had declared war on another country, and where the Farmer lived, if the Military came for your son, by law, he had to go to war. The Military Captain showed up at the Farmer's home and asked, "Your son is needed to fight in the war. Where is he?" The Farmer said, "My son is here but he can't fight, his leg is badly broken." The Military Captain fetched the town doctor and he verified that the Farmer's son's leg was indeed broken and he could not fight in the war. The Military Captain understood and left the Farmer's son alone to recuperate and not go to war.

That's when the Farmer realized that the Great Spirit had broken his son's leg to spare his son from the horrors of war. The Farmer also realized that sometimes things must be broken right now, to manifest a better life for you in the near future.

SOURCE: Justin Perry – YouTube Guru - YouAreCreators

The Moral of the Story: If you're asking life, to bring you a better life (i.e. money, a new home, a new job, a better relationship, etc.), then your current life circumstances cannot not remain the same – new things must happen to make changes to the old stuff you have in your life. Therefore, "The Grand Deconstruction" happens to clear away old life circumstances to make way for the new life you've been praying for, (oftentimes clearing the way, very dramatically). In order for the Universe to create the life that you truly desire, your old life must be busted-up and reconstructed to achieve better results. The bad will pass and give way to a positive future, if you don't give-up. Never give up and hold on to faith.

So, even though you're going through awful stuff, be patient, avoid negatively opinionated people (negative opinions slow you down, and don't pay your bills), bravely press on (life favors the bold), be positively persistent, and take positive forward actions (big or small), so that when any viable opportunities arise you can effectively capitalize on them. Quickly move into your new life with courage and love because you deserve to intentionally live a beautiful happy life! ☺

CHAPTER 20

PREGNANT FOR ALL THE WRONG REASONS

How many of us know women with small children struggling to make ends meet?

Single-mothers' live with as much dignity as they can muster but they seem to be fighting a losing financial battle because of the father or fathers are nowhere in the picture to aid the ladies with the everyday raising of their children. It's an epidemic of broken hearts, broken promises, and broken lives. **Have you ever gotten pregnant, or have gotten someone else pregnant, for all the wrong reasons?**

Wrong Reasons for Getting Pregnant:

1. **I love him/or her and I want to show my true love by having a baby.** Do Not – I repeat – Do Not bring an innocent baby into this world if you don't have all your financial eggs lined-up in a row!

   In other words, if you're a teenager or younger, and you still live with your parents or parent, don't have a baby. It's selfish, dangerous, and stupid. Love is great, but you and your baby can't eat love when you're hungry. Last time I checked love didn't pay the bills either. Bad men and boys love to get females impregnated when the females are young and easy to trick into intimacy. Why? Because triumphantly (inside some males twisted callous immature selfish minds), getting a female pregnant proves to the world that they were good enough to be intimate with you and create a baby, (especially if you're a cute innocent female).

Control through impregnation by males is a very selfish and insidious, female control technique used as an attempt to maintain forcible control over unwitting females without actually caring for the welfare of the females or their innocent babies. It's a horrible fact of everyday life that many young females bodies will be used and have their lives ruined because of unwanted pregnancies. Will you be the next victim, or victimizer? Don't get pregnant until you're a responsible adult. Mom and Dad will love you for it!

2. **I don't have anyone around who loves me so I want to have my own family.** That's a pie in the sky unrealistic fantasy. By creating a baby to feel love assures a lady a life of hardship from poor finances and bad abusive relationships. Think about it!

3. **He /or she is in a bad marriage but the married person is in love with me and not with the person he/she is married to.** Every day many people hope that the married person they're in love with is being totally honest when they tell them they will leave their significant other for them.

Only **3%** of people in marital affairs leave their spouse because of their affair. So, a marital break-up is mostly a daydream, ready to turn into a nightmare! Don't have a cute little baby with a married person it's more trouble than it's worth. There are major problems involved with having a lovechild with a married person – is it worth all the deceit and the loss of dignity?

4. **For the money!** The baby loses big in this deal. Even if you receive a big paycheck the hate and innuendo for having a baby to gold-dig money from a man will linger for decades. Ill-will between a user mother and bitter male parent wreaks havoc on the welfare of the innocent child. If that be the case, the child will never know the joy of having both parents involved positively in their life.

Please think before you act ladies. Too many children are left to suffer unspeakable horrors that can warp their fragile minds for life. Many children born into difficult situations end up suffering tremendous mental and physical abuse because their mothers and fathers are in impoverished positions that allow opportunities for child abuse to occur. A major reason for child abuse is because single-parents' can't afford safe and proper daycare for their children. I'm so tired of hearing about child abuses because of poor people having to leave a child with untrained babysitters, or people you think are trustworthy - but are in fact opportunistic male monsters, (i.e. people you think you can trust uncles, cousins, best friends, etc....). It breaks my heart, and rips families apart, but it's especially tough on the abused children. To live a better life means making choices that will leave instant gratification on the back burner. Delay gratification for a little while and please consider that it's not only your life when you have a little bundle of joy. Wait to have a baby - until the time's right. Plan your Parenthood.

CHAPTER 21

HOW TO SURVIVE
THE BREAK-UP WITH
MINIMAL GRIEF

It Finally Happens! The Break-up! Ohhh Nooooo! It Feels like I'm Going to Die! What can I do to make myself feel better - other than destroying my once beloved ex- mate's personal property (car, clothes, etc.), or killing him/or her?

Psychologist estimate mentally recovering from nasty relationship splits may take up to **4** years. Psychologists also estimate that people recover faster from a mate dying, rather than a bad break-up.   Why? Because at least the feeling of betrayal is not there and you don't have to see them walking around with someone else. Wow! Ladies and Gentlemen, 4 years is far too long to wallow in break-up suffering. Especially when there's some important living to do. Remember time waits for no one. So, what can we do when we break the relationship off? First, you must understand that the reason you feel so terrible after a break-up is because you've developed an addiction to your mate. That's right people are addicted to people! Like a person who's addicted to a mind-altering drug. Hence the expression, "Can't live with you – Can't live without you!"

FOR EXAMPLE:

We need a person to be the subject of this discussion – you reading this right now - you'll do! Hypothetically speaking of course:

Now play along please. You're a hopeless crack-cocaine addict and your favorite thing in this world is to get a big crack rock and smoke it! All day and all night! Puff-Puff! ☺ Then the person you love most in the world (let's say your mother), finds out that you have a crack cocaine habit and it's causing you to harm yourself greatly. So, your beautiful mother, in a desperate attempt of intervention to get you back on the right track, confines you to a room with an ounce of crack rock in front of you. Your mother tells you, "I love you, and this is for your own good. It hurts me more than it does you. You can't touch that crack-rock unless you agree to flush it down the toilet, and promise never to smoke crack-cocaine again!"

Now stop here and think for a minute… How would that make you feel inside?

I remind you that you're an addict, who loves to smoke cocaine more than anything in this world.   But here's your sweet loving mother. The most important love of your life, telling you that you can't touch the cocaine right before your eyes. How does that make you feel? Do you feel grateful? Do you feel angry? What are you willing to do to satisfy these powerful cravings and end the withdrawals that are taking a toll on you physically and emotionally? Would you lie? Would you plead and beg? Would you be nice and sweet? Would you be physical or forceful? Remember you're an addict and your mother won't let you take the drug sitting right before your eyes.

Now this is the way that people feel and react who are addicted to each other in relationships. Only People don't know that it's an actual addiction. Relationship or Love Addiction is also known as "Obsession". Relationship Addiction is more often as strong as an addiction to cocaine or heroin. That's why people do so many terrible things to each other - that under normal (non-addict) circumstances they would never do.

Also, people with Relationship Addiction suffer from negative physical and emotional withdrawals that cause a great deal of mental anguish in pain. Relationship addiction happens in all relationships no matter what the gender or the age of a person (i.e. kids, teens, and adults). It's either a small addiction or a large addiction but it can be especially strong when lust is involved. Even if the most important person in your life intervenes on your behalf, it won't stop the addict from attempting to get their fix (i.e. happy time with your mate). The more you love or lust for the person, the greater the withdrawal symptoms that attack your body and mind.

You go through chemical withdrawals and the brain fears that you'll not be able to supply the fix that it desperately craves. That's why people can be so cruel to one another - not realizing that what they're going through is the complex emotional disease of addiction withdrawal. Take alcohol away from an alcoholic and they will fight you to get it back. In relationships people react in a similar fashion. If I can't have my fix from my partner than no one can! That's the bad attitude that kicks in when negative emotions run high and the IQ chemical levels in the brain drops. Before you know, you've lost control of yourself and all manner of mayhem will take place. Peoples' cruel beasts of unfettered jealousy and fiery anger are unleashed onto the World - and the Passion War ensues!

I've mastered the technique of rebounding from bitter break-ups through years of personal study, trial and error, and a lot of bad relationships. Follow these helpful tips to help you ride the waves of the break-up storm and stay afloat rather than drown in emotional turmoil:

PHILOSOPHER X's RELATIONSHIP (BREAK-UP SURVIVAL GUIDE)

When the Break-Up is Done, You Need to Protect Yourself from the Stresses and Strains of (BAW) Break-Up Addiction Withdrawal

Step 1. Remove any visible pictures of your EX and put them in a safe place. Do not take phone calls from your EX or visit places where you might run into your EX. Do this for up to **3** months. *The exception to this rule is if you're going to take your EX back. If not, stick to the three-month rule and it's ok to let your EX-know that you're not going to be talking to him/or her for a while.*

Step 2. Get an over-the-counter sleep remedy to help you sleep through the night - natural or medicinal. Thinking about your EX may disrupt your ability to sleep. Lack of sleep causes major stress.

Step 3. Hang out with family and friends in fun places that will make you laugh. Laughter is the best medicine for combating BAW. Keep these friends and relatives initially on standby at in the beginning stages of the Break-Up for at least the next 3 to 4 weeks for support.

Step 4. Watch only Movies and TV programs that make you laugh, and listen to music that makes you want to dance - for the next three to four weeks. Don't watch any horrors or intense dramas, as you need to keep the feel-good opiates elevated in your brain.

Step 5. Treat yourself to all your favorite foods, snacks and drinks, (coffee, tea, soda, wine, cake, etc.). Keep away from consuming large amounts of alcohol. If the treats you eat are fattening - that's ok! Just do your favorite exercises later to compensate for the extra calories. This keeps the opiate levels up in the brain and eases the effects of BAW. This will help you get over this troubling state of mind in as little as three months rather than two to four years.

Step 6. After you've had time to heal your mind, body, and soul, start getting back on a healthy diet and when you're ready - find a new more compatible mate. If love doesn't work out with the new person - repeat steps 1 through 6 again. ☺

There you have it! A sure-fire way to bounce back to a peaceful state of mind after the break-up. This technology enables you to faster live life happily again. Your EX's will wonder how you bounced back so fast without pining away for them. This technique works so use it if you must and pass the knowledge on. Pay It Forward! All the relationship facts I've shared with you thus far has revealed the ultimate-ultimate truths about the makings of human relationships. Now that you know, what are you willing to compromise to have a happy, peaceful, and successful relationship?

CHAPTER 22

COMPROMISING

At last you've found that special someone that has enough positive hits on the Mr. Right or Ms. Right list and you want to take the next big step with him/or her. Commitment! The C-word can be an elusive prospect in the world of relationships but it's as inevitable as a visit by the Grim Reaper or the IRS tax service. That's if the relationship is going to last for a while! Commitment can be in many varying degrees as some people are more comfortable with committing to relationships than others. The important thing is to have a clear understanding of what level of commitment you're willing to settle for.

Commitment is a binding verbal or written contractual agreement between willing parties that hope that the committed person will stick to the deal and positively enhance their personal life. That's right being in relationships is like running a business! Now prepare yourselves for the most honest and unorthodox approach ever created to get to the crux of what's acceptable in your Relationships:

THE COMPROMISE SCALE

Relationships are rarely easy, and the more you honestly know about each other at the very beginning of your mutual endeavor, the better off you'll be in the long run.

Knowing each other increases the possibility of creating a loving and successful relationship. Remember that all relationships are experiments and you're the scientist gathering information to bring about the best possible desired results. I recommend that you create copies of the Compromise Scale and fill it out yourself first. Then keep the copies you create for yourself secretly. Remember you can always change your answers but stay honest with yourself when you do.

In time give the Compromise Scale to your prospective mate to complete (keeping your own Compromise Scale a secret), and continue to keep each other's Compromise Scales' a secret until you're both ready to meet in private to discuss the parameters of your future relationship. If the prospective mate does not wish to participate in filling out the Compromise Scale, then it's probably just better to just remain friends. Don't be frightened to follow through on any actions needed to satisfy your understanding of your relationship situation. Be courageous and complete this exercise. This scale is also great for couples who are already married or in committed relationships. It's ok for all participants to re-do the compromise scale from time to time because people may change as they age:

COMPROMISE SCALE – (Feel Free to Modify Questions – As Needed)

1. Do you want to be in a committed relationship? If so what type of commitment? If not, what type of relationship would you like?

2. When was the last time you were in a relationship? Do you still have contact with your ex? If so what type of feelings do you have for your ex?

3. Are you married? Have you ever been married? If so for how long and why did it end? Do you have to pay alimony or child support?

4. Do you have children? If so how many? Do you have a relationship with your children if so how do you participate? Do you mind if I have children?

5. What activities do you like to do to have fun? What are your favorite hobbies? Are you willing to try new things?

6. What religion are you? Are you open to exploring or participating in different religious possibilities?

7. What's your current age, height, nationality, and weight?

8. Do you drink alcohol, smoke tobacco products, smoke illegal drugs, or do any kind of illegal drugs? If so how long and how much do you use? Are you willing to go to professional therapy to quit if necessary?

9. Do you take prescription drugs? If so why and how much?

10. What's your political party? Would it be a problem if I am in a different political party?

11. Can you cook? If so what's your best dish? How much do you enjoy cooking? What foods do you dislike/or hate eating?

12. Are you close to your family? If so how close? If not, why? When can I meet your family?

13. Do you have a job? If so what is it? If not, why? How much income do you make a year? Are you comfortable with me seeing a copy of your credit report? Are you willing to pitch in financially if needed?

14. How is your health on a scale of 1 to 10 (1 the lowest 10 the highest)? Do you work out?

15. Do you have any STD's (Sexually Transmitted Diseases), if so explain how they affect your life? Are you willing to get checked for STD's and not take it as a personal insult?

16. Do you practice safe intimacy, if so in what way?

17. How important is intimacy to you in a relationship on a scale of 1 to 10 (1 the lowest 10 the highest)?

18. How often do you expect to have intimacy in a relationship once it starts?

19. If we ever agree to have intimacy are you willing to be attentive to my needs in and be open to discussion or instruction without being offended?

20. Are you jealous? If so now much on a scale of 1 to 10 (1 the lowest 10 the highest)?

21. I have male and female friends would you trust me to hang out with them from time to time without being angry, disrespectful, or abusive to me?

22. Is it ok to go to a male/or female strip club with friends from time to time without you being angry, disrespectful, or abusive to me?

23. Do you have a felony crime on your record? If so explain what and why?

24. Are you willing to provide information to allow me to do a background check without being offended?

25. Would you defend me if I encountered trouble not of my doing? If so how?

26. What are your plans for your own future?

27. What do you want from a mate in a relationship?

28. How many children would you like to have if we marry and are you open to adoption?

29. If we decide to marry are you open to signing a legal pre-nuptial agreement without being offended?

30. If we decide to marry are you open to pre-marital counseling before marriage and counseling during marriage if we're having marital problems?

WHAT STYLE OF COMMITMENT ARE YOU OPEN TO?

- Male with multiple wives

- Wife with multiple males

- Man and wife open marriage, with shared or unshared partners

- Committed relationship without lawful marriage

- Traditional one man - one woman marriage

- Friend with benefits (with/or without the possibility of commitment? Re-evaluate this option every six months)

Pick the commitment style you feel most important to you right now? Hint: You can pick more than one to compromise.

a. If you are open to multiple partners how would you like for it to be set-up, and what participation is fair to you?

b. If children are to be a part of our marriage would you still fell the same way about your chosen commitment style?

c. What do you consider a deal-breaker in a committed relationship?

d. **If our compromise models don't match it's best we agree to just be friends.**

Now that you have a better understanding of what you're dealing with in your potential mate - feel free to check out any information you need to move forward with your relationship.

WARNING: Do not let anyone copy or keep your compromise scale paperwork! Especially the person you're negotiating with! It can and will be used against you in a Court of Law!

CHAPTER 23

ADOPTIONS

You're happy in your dream relationship and now you want to start a family of your on. Have you ever considered Adoption?

Adoption of a child is a gift, and it's something that's needed in our world. Now more than ever! Overpopulation is becoming a real threat given that for most of human history the numbers of people walking on the planet were only a few thousand - to a few million. So, resources like food, water, medicine, shelter, and energy are becoming scarcer. Now there's over seven billion people on this planet and growing! Scientists and ecologists believe that we are eroding the world's resources to fast to maintain the current population and this could threaten humans with extinction. Sadly, limited food and a lack of clean water are causing a lot of innocent lives to be lost to the ravages of starvation. It's estimated that 30,000 people die of complications derived from starvation daily, most of them children. That's a child hopelessly and needlessly dying every second of every day.

THE ADOPTION PROJECT

Several years ago, as I contemplated what we could do as people to make the world a better place, I gathered that taking care of our orphaned children could help save a lot of innocent lives. Even if you can't adopt you can contribute to orphanages or some other type of necessary child care to save young lives. What I'm asking people to do is to consider reducing the rate of overpopulation by agreeing to adopt your first child and if you already have a first child, instead of birthing your second child adopt one instead. One of the biggest reasons people have a second child is because they want to add a boy or a girl to the family, and usually if the second child is not the boy or girl you want - you keep trying. You may get the boy or girl on the first try if you're lucky! With adoption, the gender is certain, and the grateful child will love you forever. ☺

Let's adopt a child and in the process, save some wear and tear on your significant others lovely body, not to mention saving the planet from overpopulation. I know people who have adopted children, including my own family, and they love those children as if they birthed them themselves. Also, the new siblings love the adopted children as well. It's a beautiful thing! We must break away from the old norms of only caring for our own biological babies if we're ever going to create a better world for us to live.

Adopt a child and create a world that you'll be proud to live in together! ☺

CONCLUSION

The Living Life Equation ~ By: Philosopher 'X'

> In life, you live in sporadic moments of Peace – You attempt to live peacefully for as long as you possibly can, (i.e. peace of mind, happiness, satisfaction, and contentment).

> Then you suffer disruptions to your Peace, this happens when problems occur, (i.e. money issues, relationship issues, health issues).

> Then you seek to cure or alleviate the offending problem or problems - as quickly as possible - so that you can return to living a Peaceful Existence.

> Attempting to return to Peace fast, you use the education you have acquired over your lifetime - or you seek aid and advice from others. So, that hopefully you can end the problem to your Peace hastily. The quicker you return to Peace - the more time you spend living a wonderful happy life.

> Once the problem is solved you return to "Peace of Mind" again.

That's the Living Life Equation Cycle
- It Forever Repeats!

"The fact of the matter is, that if you're continuously having undesired hardships in your relationships there's something about yourself that you need to reflect on and correct. Work On Improving Yourself."

Philosopher 'X'

"What your mind believes, you create as reality in your life."

Hypnotherapist - Marisa Peer – Mind Valley Institute

Relationship problems give us a lesson about life that's being overlooked or ignored. Relationships are a litmus test that needs and demands our serious attention if we are to become better people in life. Relationships are our mirrors of ourselves. No man, woman, or child that you let in your life will be able to fix what's keeping you in a repeat awful relationship mode. You're the only one who can end your series of disastrous conclusions within your relationships. Please understand that by far, the most important relationship you can ever have – is with yourself. Your world begins and ends with you so you're responsible for creating the circumstances in your life - for better, or for worse. The sooner you believe this fact the better. **(I strongly recommend you look at YouTube videos by Michael Bernard Beckwith).**

Get to know yourself, so that you truly know what's important to you, and how best to approach your wants, needs, and desires without someone else making those decisions for you. It's your life, your body, and your spirit, that's being affected. You can't turn back the hands of time so when your life is done - it's done. Live your life fully with courageous conviction! Educate yourself and follow your will. You and only you can control your fate. **When an Adult Man or Woman, gives another person the full authoritative power to guide their life (i.e. Authority figures, Wife, Husband, etc.), the <u>prolonged</u> control will always end up in 'Abusive Behavior' being perpetrated against them! No matter how noble the intentions. If you're an Adult and you let another adult take control of over your daily life that makes you their slave!** Don't give your life and power over to anyone. No matter what. Sure, you may lose some relationships by not kowtowing to a megalomaniac, but you won't be suffering unnecessarily as life passes you by. Get out of bad abusive relationships because life's too short. Stand-up for yourself, think for yourself, and live a life that you will be proud of. Trust me it's worth the effort.

"There's more to life than the chase - every action between a man and a woman doesn't have to be a ploy to have intimacy, even if the man or woman finds the other attractive in a desirable way. How will you ever be able to connect to the spirit of a person if your mind is a prisoner of its own flesh?"

Quote ~ Philosopher 'X'

LIFE IS A TRAIN RIDE

Life is like a journey on a train...with its stations...with changes of routes...and with accidents…

🚂🚃🚃🚃🚃

We board this train when we are born and our parents are the ones who get our ticket.

🚂🚃🚃🚃🚃

We believe they will always travel on this train with us.

🚂🚃🚃🚃🚃

However, at some station our parents will get off the train, leaving us alone on this journey.

🚂🚃🚃🚃🚃

As time goes by, other passengers will board the train, many of whom will be significant - our siblings, friends, children, and even the love of our life.

🚂🚃🚃🚃🚃

Many will get off during the journey and leave a permanent vacuum in our lives.

🚂🚃🚃🚃🚃

Many will go so unnoticed that we won't even know when they vacated their seats and got off the train.

🚂🚃🚃🚃🚃

This train ride will be full of joy, sorrow, fantasy, expectations, hellos, good-byes, and farewells.

A good journey is helping, loving, having a good relationship with all co-passengers... and making sure that we give our best to make their journey comfortable.

The mystery of this fabulous journey is: We do not know at which station we ourselves are going to get off.

So, we must live in the best way - adjust, forget, forgive and offer the best of what we have.

It is important to do this because when the time comes for us to leave our seat... we should leave behind beautiful memories for those who will continue to travel on the train of life.

Thank you for being one of the important passengers on my train... don't know when my station will come... don't want 2 miss saying: "Thank you"

Source: Anonymous Beautiful Person on the Net

I hope you found that the contents of this book gave you some helpful insights into the world of relationships. I also hope that you're now able to look at your relationships with people in more creative ways than ever before. That you'll be able to put away "foolish pride" by attempting to always be right and never wrong in your relationship interactions. It's always been said that "Pride Goeth Before the Fool!" So, don't be a fool and ruin a perfectly good relationship because you refuse to COMPROMISE between you and your loved one. Don't Be Stuck on Stupid!

My greatest wish is that you find happiness and total fulfillment in all your relationships from this point onwards.

I, Philosopher 'X,' - look forward to creating a more peaceful, beautiful, and joyful world with you.

I'm truly thankful for that possibility! XOXO ☺
Philosopher 'X'

Be At Peace, Be Happy, and Have a Great Life!

SINCERELY, PHILOSOPHER 'X' ☺

www.ingramcontent.com/pod-product-compliance
Lightning Source LLC
Chambersburg PA
CBHW052000090426
42741CB00008B/1475